ONTARIO
forests

ONTARIO
forests

A Historical Perspective

K. A. ARMSON R.P.F. B.Sc.F.

ONTARIO
FORESTRY
ASSOCIATION

Fitzhenry & Whiteside
Toronto, Ontario

Ontario Forests

Copyright © 2001 Ontario Forestry Association

Published by Fitzhenry and Whiteside Limited, 195 Allstate Parkway, Markham, Ontario L3R 4T8, www.fitzhenry.ca godwit@fitzhenry.ca ; and the Ontario Forestry Association, 200 Consumers Road, Suite 307, Toronto, Ontario M2J 4R4, www.oforest.on.ca forestry@oforest.on.ca .

Fitzhenry & Whiteside acknowledges with thanks the Canada Council for the Arts, the Government of Canada through its Book Publishing Industry Development Program, and the Ontario Arts Council for their support of our publishing program.

Canadian Cataloguing in Publication Data

Armson, K.A., 1927–
    Ontario forests: a historical perspective

Co-published by Ontario Forestry Association.
Includes bibliographical references and index.
ISBN 1-55041-626-X

1. Forests and forestry–Ontario–History. I. Ontario Forestry Association. II. Title.

SD146.O5A75 2001   577.3'09713   C00-933050-X

Design by Karen Petherick, Intuitive Design International Ltd.
Cover images courtesy of Algonquin Provincial Park Museum

Printed and bound in Canada

The following drawings and silhouettes - conifer family (page 56); broadleaf family (page 57); white spruce (page 59); black spruce (page 61); jack pine, red pine (page 62); eastern white pine, balsam fir (page 63); white cedar (page 64); trembling aspen (page 66); white birch (page 67); sugar maple (page 68); white oak, white elm (page 69); basswood, black ash (page 71); and balsam poplar, black walnut (page 73) are copyright the Canadian Forestry Service, National Resources Canada, and have been reproduced with permission from *Trees of Canada* by John Laird Farrar, with permission of the Minister of Public Works and Government Services Canada, 2001.

*"In North America, still close to its pioneer days and ways
the forest has been so close to us, has affected our individual and
communal lives so deeply, that to the minds of those who fall
under its spell it seems to have been much more than an
impersonal form of nature. Like the sea, it is apt to seduce
its familiars from the matter-of-fact and to levy imaginative tribute."*

*(A.R.M.Lower in
The North American Assault on the Canadian Forest, 1938)*

Table of Contents

K. A. Armson

Acknowledgements

This is not a history of forests and forestry in Ontario, I leave that to the professional historians, but rather the perspective of one forester looking back on the forest scene in the province and how it has changed over time. Inevitably, I have drawn not only on my own experiences over more than 50 years, but the influences, information and insights I have gained from colleagues and others during this period. In particular I would acknowledge the many discussions I had, both as a student and then fellow staff member, with Dean J.W.B. (Bernie) Sisam, and professors T. (Teddy) W. Dwight, R. (Bob) C. Hosie, D. (Dave) V. Love, and A. (Art) S. Michell, at the Faculty of Forestry, University of Toronto. During my tenure at the University of Toronto, and then with the Ontario Ministry of Natural Resources, I was associated with many foresters, forest technicians and others in universities, governments and the forest industry and to them, collectively, I owe a debt of gratitude for their indulgence and help in giving me some insight into their contribution to Ontario's forests and forestry.

In the writing of this book I have turned to a few specific persons for their advice and assistance. In particular, I would acknowledge the help and courtesy of Bob Staley and Bill Smith for allowing me to use them and the forests they manage in the Prologue. A number of staff at the Ministry of Natural Resources were particularly helpful; I am grateful for the advice of Peter Hynard on the former Minden Crown Management Unit, Andrew Jano for searching out landsat imagery, the assistance of Larry Watkins for providing forest inventory data and graphics, Wasyl Bakowsky for the information on the savannahs and prairies of Ontario, and Paul Ward for the data on forest fires. Gordon Howse and Richard Macnaughton of the Great Lakes Forestry Centre (Canadian Forest Service) provided data on spruce budworm and photos of tree diseases, respectively. Pauline Beggs and Lisa Hilderley of First Folio converted my rough drawings into first class illustrations, and the Ontario Archaeological Society and Dr. William D. Finlayson, former Director-General of the London

Museum of Archaeology, helped with information on pre-European peoples. Mark Kuhlberg, as an historian, has provided me with much insight into the early days of the pulp and paper companies and their relations with government in Ontario. John Cary gave me his constructive, critical review of Chapters V and VI, for which I am most grateful. Finally, I want to thank Erik Turk and the Ontario Forestry Association for support in the publication of this book.

Unless there is an acknowledgement, the photos are from my slide collection. I would specifically acknowledge the source for Figure 4-2, it was: "Reprinted from the Journal of Forestry (Vol.93, no.7, p.40) published by the Society of American Foresters, 5400 Grosvenor Lane, MD 20814-2198. Not for further reproduction." Permission to use Figure 5-22 was kindly provided by the University of Toronto Press.

Ken Armson,
Toronto, August, 2000

K. A. Armson

It's not every day that the student is asked to provide a preface for the teacher's book, especially when the student and teacher have disagreed publicly. But such is my opportunity here. And I am honoured, because there is no one person more exceptionally qualified to provide a historical perspective on Ontario's forests than Ken Armson. All of us who are concerned about the conservation of our forests—environmental activists, forest industry representatives, scientists, aboriginal peoples, professional foresters, policy makers, students, in fact the full spectrum of citizens from every walk of life—can be grateful that Ken has taken advantage of his lifetime career to set this history down for those who come after.

I first met Professor Armson in the mid-seventies, when I was a graduate student in forestry at the University of Toronto. He was already a noted authority on silviculture, he had written the textbook on forest soils, and he was in the process of finishing his 1976 report *Forest Management in Ontario*, commissioned by the Ministry of Natural Resources. Ken used his silviculture courses to share and discuss the ideas which eventually appeared in his report. This gave us, as students, a unique opportunity to debate concepts that would become central to the future of forestry in Ontario, specifically the introduction of Forest Management Agreements and the 1979 Crown Timber Act.

During these lively discussions, of course, I was often the infuriating "odd man out." For example, I well remember one carefully prepared, two-hour lecture on pesticides when Ken polled the class before and after his presentation to see who still had serious reservations about these chemicals. When I was the only one to raise my hand afterwards, he smiled patiently and quipped, "Well you're not persuadable in any case, Hummel, so I have succeeded!"

To his credit, when Professor Armson was invited by the Minister of the day to take practical responsibility for *implementing* the recommendations he had made in his report, Ken bravely accepted, and eventually became Chief Forester of Ontario.

Here I go disagreeing again, but I think Ken Armson is too modest in his first sentence of *Ontario Forests* when he claims, "This is not a history of forests and forestry in Ontario…but rather the perspective of one forester looking back." Damn it, this *is* a history of Ontario's forests and forestry, and one which will endure. Yes, it inevitably reflects the author's point of view, but it also contains a wealth of geological, historical and silvicultural facts that all of us need, in order to engage intelligently in discussions about the future. And Armson's point of view is well worth keeping in mind—that forests are fundamentally dynamic, that what we see on the landscape today should never be conceived as freeze-framed, but understood as the product of both natural and human history. And, of course, the forest *continues* to change as such.

My favorite sentence in this book is that our perceptions are coloured by "an individual's experiences and memories of trees and forests—the sights and smells and activities associated with them." I'm sure this rings true for the industrial forester and naturalist alike, and it nicely captures my own experience with a patch of forest personally important to me, namely 270 acres of mixed hardwoods and wonderfully regenerating white pine which I own on the Canadian Shield.

My forest will be "protected," which in Armson's terms means it will change at the hand of nature, for 999 years, thanks to a conservation agreement with The Nature Conservancy of Canada. Ironically, these same lands once belonged to renowned timber baron E.W. Rathbun. But I'm reminded, in this book, that Rathbun is also the man who in 1899 chaired a Royal Commission on Forestry which posed a question as relevant today as it was then: "What should be our proper course in utilizing forest products and in preserving the productive power of our forests?"

I've often wondered if E. W. Rathbun ever actually walked in my woods, and if so what were the "sights, smells, experiences and memories" he associated with them? Whatever they were, my forest is his legacy, just as tomorrow's forest will be mine.

Exactly Ken Armson's point.

Monte Hummel
President
World Wildlife Fund Canada
August, 2000

K. A. Armson

Introduction

Forests and trees have been an integral part of the history of mankind. They have provided food, warmth, and shelter, entered into our cultural life, and as J.G. Frazer[1] has comprehensively described, religious and spiritual activities and experiences for many races and cultures throughout the world have related to trees and woods. Forests and the other resources of wildlife, plants, soils and minerals they contain have been, and continue to be the source of economic and social development in many parts of the world. Too often the results of such activities have resulted in destruction not only of forests but changed, often irreparably, the nature of the landscape in which they occurred. From the times of the Phoenicians, trading in timber from the Mediterranean forests, to the present, the pattern of clearing and depletion has been too common. Yet it would be wrong to assume that these and later societies did not have or employ practices of husbandry, land management and utilization that were founded upon under-standing the requirements and limitations of soil and location in maintaining forests. Human history is replete with examples of where applications of the knowledge and experiences embodied in such practices and management have succumbed to wars, pesti-lence, greed, emotion and irrational behaviour. It is not surprising that similar mixes of individual and societal decisions and actions have been factors in Ontario's and Canada's forests.

Ontario's forest lands of 69 million hectares constitute 65% of a total area of 107 million hectares. The province owns 88% of the forest land; 11% is privately owned and the remaining 1% is in federal ownership. Despite the preponderance of forest lands, the majority of Ontario's population of 12 million reside in towns and cities, primarily in southern Ontario. Historically, with agricultural and then industrial development over the past two centuries the forests have been viewed in many different ways. However, two hundred years is but a small segment of time in the overall period in which forests and people have existed in Ontario, and it is within the broader time-frame beginning with the last retreat of the continental glacier that covered all of this province up to the present that this story is about.

Forests are many things to different people. Not only are there the cultural and spiritual-religious aspects that colour perceptions but more prosaically an individual's experiences and memories of trees and forests—the sights and smells and activities associated with them. What then, is a forest? Technically or scientifically, it is defined as a plant community predominantly of trees and other woody vegetation, growing more or less closely together. For most people this omits many of the features they associate with forests and with their perceptions of forests. Often, when a person speaks of a forest, the listener assumes it is defined by some known interest of the speaker. For example, a forest industry person is often assumed to consider a forest only in terms of merchantable timber, or a hunter in terms of game animals. Unfortunately these assumptions have become caricatures that are then portrayed as representative of a particular person's or sector's position with respect to the use of forests. As always there are exceptions but for most persons, whatever their particular interest or background, when they speak of a "forest" it invariably connotes much more than just a collection of trees. Yet it is the trees which give the forest its structure and in so doing determine to a very great degree the conditions for other plants and animals. This is the reason why we commonly describe forests primarily in terms of their tree component, yet with a clear understanding that we include all the organisms and processes associated therein.

Perceptions of forests by individuals and by society are also affected by information from many sources, a main one being the results of studies by scientists and professionals in biology and applied sciences such as forestry. Concepts that are developed from such studies and then given prominence in the media are too often misunderstood or misapplied to specific situations. The words and notions associated with them such as, *ecosystem*, *biodiversity* and *sustainability* are now commonplace, and any consideration of Ontario's forests must invoke their use, and for this reason they are discussed here.

K. A. Armson

The Land Base

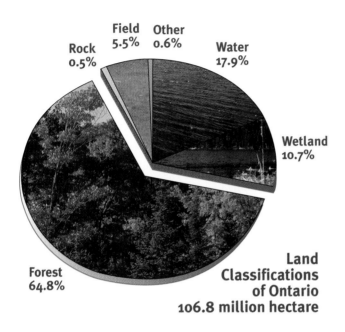

Rock
0.5%

Field
5.5%

Other
0.6%

Water
17.9%

Wetland
10.7%

Forest
64.8%

**Land
Classifications
of Ontario
106.8 million hectare**

Land Class	Areas in thousands ('ooo's) of hectares
Water – inland	10,175.3
Water – Great Lakes	8,886.9
Wetland – marsh/bog/fen	11,418.3
Wetland – forested – treed bog and fen	14,169.2
Conifer forest (softwoods)	23,817.4
Broadleaved forest (hardwoods)	8,586.0
Mixedwood forest	15,421.5
Disturbed forest – fire and harvested	7,280.8
Rock	548.3
Field and Agriculture	5,854.2
Other – roads, towns, cities etc	641.9
Total	106,800.0

A feature of forests and the organisms associated with them is the element of change that occurs not only over the short term of days, weeks and months but those that take place, often slowly, over the longer term of years, decades and centuries. This feature of change often distorts or is ignored in the beliefs or remembrances that people have of forests. Trees and all the other living organisms grow, change their size and shape, and in so doing alter the conditions around them. What is equally important is that they alter their own demands for light, moisture, nutrients, and temperature, and the processes involved in their supply. By modifying the conditions around them, they affect other organisms, some of which may be dependent on them. Conceptually, the mental consideration of organisms in relation to their environment, including other organisms and the non-living components, at whatever level or scale, as an *ecosystem* was first suggested by an English botanist, A.G. Tansley in 1935. In this sense it is any organism or group of organisms and the systems and processes associated with them that may be chosen or isolated for purposes of study. It is essentially a concept for intellectual application. In recent years, particularly in North America, the use of the word ecosystem has become warped to refer to specific communities, and all the components biotic and abiotic that exist on a defined area (i.e. spatially explicit, and for many, virtually fixed in time). Given that conceptually or with spatial dimensions, an ecosystem is dynamic, never static, the expression "preservation of an ecosystem" is an oxymoron and serves to mislead rather than realistically describe a forest condition and its properties. In this book, "ecosystem" will be used in its original sense and not as an unnecessary appellation to every type of forest. For example, a forest will be identified as a "jack pine forest," not a "jack pine forest ecosystem." It is understood that the former, shorter label and the forest it is applied to, is a dynamic complex of organisms and processes but is objectively defined, and time dependent.

The growth of living organisms such as trees is an incremental process. Ultimately and usually as a result of a combination or culmination of causes, the organisms will decline and eventually die. The character and nature of the space they occupied will change, sometimes with a renewal of the species that died or often its replacement by other species. The sequential change in a forest from one specified type to another is termed *succession*. When the pattern of succession is determined for a sequence of specific forest

K. A. Armson

types and conditions, that knowledge may be used to predict the nature of the future forest. As with all predictions there is no certainty, only probabilities; unexpected aberrant factors especially disturbances can alter the nature of succession.

Although the development of organisms and the biological, physical and chemical processes associated with it are continuous for the most part, the forests of Canada and Ontario have been and still are subjected to major disturbances or *perturbations* that can dramatically change the forest and the land on which it occurs. Forest fires, tornado-force winds, floods, insect and disease infestations, and human activities are the major sources of such disturbances. Often they occur in combination or sequence. Defoliations by insects of one tree species can change the growing conditions for other species, and render a forest more susceptible to fire. Human clearing of the forest for cultivation or the residual slash left from a logging operation can result in fires that burn surrounding forests. Flooding either from non-human or human causes, such as clearing forest lands for agriculture, can profoundly change both vegetation and existing drainage patterns. Too often the effects of a disturbance, such as forest fire, and expected succession are portrayed as being the same no matter where they occur. Some effects may be similar but often vary in degree. Generally, however, the effects of major disturbances are highly variable depending on their magnitude, intensity, frequency, and duration. It is in this light that any attempt must be made to rationalize the features of an existing forest in relation to its past history and disturbance. Thus a major emphasis in this book is on the history of Ontario's lands and forests over time, since the retreat of the last glacier, and the nature of the factors which have resulted in the forests we see today.

There is always diversity in a forest, no matter how uniform it may appear to the eye. The concept of *biodiversity* is used to describe three aspects of diversity: ecosystems, species, and genetic properties for specific communities. As with the concept of ecosystem, the term's application to any specific ecosystem, species or genetic attributes necessitates defining in precise and quantifiable terms what measures of diversity are to be used. This is important because often from an apparent visual 'sameness' or lack of diversity in the tree component it may be concluded, wrongly, that there is minimal biodiversity. It is also too often wrongly assumed that there is some specific static state of biodiversity for any given area.

1

Forested — Productive and Non-Productive Lands by Ownership
Areas in thousands ('ooo's) of hectares

Class	Ontario Crown			Federal	Private	Total
Forested	**Parks & Reserves**	**Other**	**Total**			
Productive	4,570	29,032	33,602	484	5,527	39,613
Non-Productive (muskeg, brush, rock)	582	4,782	5,364	64	644	6,072
Totals	5,152	33,814	38,966	548	6,171	45,685

2

Forested Lands by Ownership
Areas in thousands of hectares

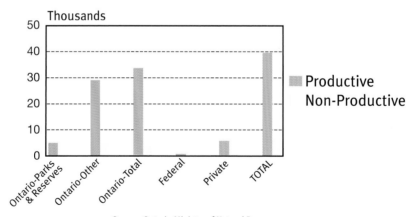

Source: Ontario Ministry of Natural Resources

Inventoried Forest Lands — Ownership

N.B. Of the total area of the province (106,800,000 hectares), 59,715,181 hectares are included in the Forest Resources Inventory (FRI), 1996, as up-dated in 1999, and form the basis for the data in these tables. The area not included in the FRI is that of the Northern Boreal forest and Barrens north of a line approximately from 500 N at the Ontario-Québec border to 520 N at the Ontario-Manitoba border.

K. A. Armson

The state of any forest is dynamic; in addition, factors which affect the presence or absence of certain species may have no relationship to the conditions pertaining to that forest. For example, significant changes in migratory bird populations apparently associated with some measurable change in the forest, may well be attributable to factors in another part of the bird's range. Any measure of biodiversity is relative and not absolute, and must be linked to the physical setting in which it is considered. Thus the nature of the landscapes and associated physical features on which Ontario's forests have developed are of particular interest, since they affect to greater or lesser degree a species' occurrence.

Inherent in any consideration of forests, in addition to the recognition of space and time, is that of scale. When a forest is viewed at the ground level, we see trees and other organisms at a scale of 1:1. As we look around, we may recognize that there is some consistency in the species and structure of the aggregation of trees and other vegetation. Further, if we walk through this forest, we may well be able to identify where the similarity ceases. It is important to recognize that the criterion for determining similarity has to be explicit; too often it is either unstated or assumed. An area of forest containing a contiguous group of similar plants and structure we term, arbitrarily, a *stand*. The stand is a basic forest unit, and a forest is a collection of stands. When we look at stands at the ground level it is at one scale; when we look at stands at the forest level we are using a different scale. Common scales used in describing and measuring many features of forests are 1:10,000 to 1:20,000—the scales most commonly used with aerial photographs. Larger scales of 1:2,000 or 1:5,000 may be used for particular features such as the measurement of young stands. Portrayals of forests at smaller scales of 1:100,000 or less (e.g. 1:100,000,000) are used at regional, provincial or national levels to show broad forest conditions. The identification of scale is particularly important when the measure, image of a forest condition, or attribute at one scale is then used or extrapolated to the same area at some other scale. Not only are such extrapolations largely unwarranted from a technical or scientific standpoint, they can be the source of much misinformation. Thus the forest level or scale at which a particular property or attribute is measured or described is critical. This is of particular importance when attempts are made to estimate biodiversity.

The Boreal forest region of 29,672,200 hectares is approximately three times the area of the Great Lakes – St. Lawrence region and Deciduous region combined—10,630,400 hectares.

The concept of *sustainability* came into vogue following the publication of, "Our Common Future"[2]. Sustainable development was defined as the ability to, *"meet the needs of the present without compromising the ability of future generations to meet their own needs."* As with the other two concepts, ecosystem and biodiversity, sustainability is a human construct and therefore subject to a wide range of social, economic and cultural conditions—to say nothing of a given state of scientific knowledge and technological innovation. It is inevitable therefore that there will be a wide range of opinions on what sustainability is, let alone how it is to be achieved. Thus while the concept is clear, the manner of its accomplishment is largely a matter of debate. A contributing factor is that the "what" to be sustained is often described as "values," frequently in subjective or non-measurable terms. Sustainability has no meaning unless the what-where-when-how-who components of its implementation are identified. Hence the notion of "sustaining forests" is vacuous unless accompanied by specific objectives and a rationale for implementation of activities to meet those objectives in both the short and long terms, while achieving the values desired. What is really at the core of sustainability is human commitment and the associated actions required to achieve "sustainable development." In order to begin this process and apply it to forests it is obligatory to start with a complete-as-possible description or inventory of what exists, particularly the land base itself and how it came to be.

The unconsolidated mineral and organic materials which constitute the earth's surface are not uniform either in makeup or thickness, but rather the result of many forces at work over long periods of time. The most obvious feature is surface—flat, hilly, steep and so on—in other words *topography*. Topography and the materials that occur within, make up what is termed the *physiography* of the landscape. Beneath this, to greater or lesser depths, lie the bedrocks of the province. The nature of these geological and physiographic materials, their origin and the geologic forces that have formed or deposited them provide the most stable components on which any forest occurs and significantly influences how that forest may develop. Historically these materials have also influenced the nature of human occupation and use of forest lands. They constitute the medium in which trees and other vegetation are rooted; indeed the definition of soil is, *"The unconsolidated material on the immediate surface of the earth that serves as a*

K. A. Armson

natural medium for the growth of land plants."[3] For this reason the geological history of Ontario provides the setting in which forests are considered. The early development of the tree species which now form our forests, the period that their genetic makeup was mainly determined, took place long before any human activity. Two components—the development of the land base, and the nature and distribution of forest species, form the canvas on which human activities for the past 12,000 or more years have taken place and have created the picture of the forest we see now. The extent and level of those activities have increased from the days of the first indigenous peoples to the arrival of Europeans in increasingly large numbers up to the present. It is the collective effect of human and non-human influences that has led to the forests we see around us today. Throughout, the forests have been both a driver and been driven in the social, economic and ecological complexes created by each society over time.

This book is an attempt to view Ontario's forests with a historical perspective and convey a sense of the magnificent resource they have been, are, and may continue to be in the future. How that resource is sustained and the benefits it can bring is almost entirely dependent on a society that is now literally out-of-touch with the concept of forest, or which sees it only in passing moments of a few days during travel or recreation. If this book can bring a deeper knowledge and understanding of the forests and what has made them what they are, then its purpose will have been served.

II

Prologue

ſouthern Ontario

Bob Staley is a professional forester who lives on his own woodlot in the Town of Whitchurch-Stouffville, about 50 km north of Toronto. The woodlot is eight and a quarter hectares in area, of which half is hardwood forest on deep sandy soils, with a cold water stream running through the property. Staley's property is representative of much of the woodlands in the area. The trees are mainly broadleaved species of sugar maple, white ash, red oak, basswood and black cherry, with smaller amounts of white and yellow birch, American beech, poplar, ironwood, bitternut hickory and butternut. Eastern white pine is the main conifer together with lesser numbers of eastern hemlock, eastern white-cedar, tamarack, and white spruce. When Bob goes into his woodlot, either to look around and enjoy it, or to undertake some management activity such as marking trees for a future harvest, or pruning eastern white pine crop trees, he subconsciously relates what he sees today with the knowledge of a host of events that have led to the woodland that now exists.

Forester Bob Staley in his woodlot.

Photo courtesy of Bob Staley

The property is situated on sands and gravels that washed off two huge lobes of the continental ice sheet about 12 to 13 thousand years ago. The materials, as they were deposited between the two lobes, stretched in an irregular band 250 to 350 metres above sea level in an east-west direction for almost 100 km, and up to 11 km at its widest point. The formation is called the *Oak Ridges Moraine* and forms the height of land between Lake Simcoe to the north and Lake Ontario to the south. On the lower parts of the moraine there are capping layers of clay, laid down when water formed small lakes or pondings along the edge of the sands and gravels. For the most part well drained, the soils are fertile for most trees and other vegetation, but when they are exposed they can erode severely.

When the ice front left the area, the climate was very cold and only tundra-like vegetation such as dwarf, open grown spruce and willows survived where Bob's woodlot now stands. As the ice retreated farther north, the climate warmed and organic material—litter—formed a surface layer or forest floor, and dead roots from the vegetation became incorporated in the soil. Spruce forests were succeeded by eastern white, red and jack pines, poplars, birches and the associated shrubs and herbaceous vegetation that we find in such forests today. These were then followed by the maples, ashes and oaks that abound in the woodlot now, so that by three to four thousand years ago, the forest probably would have had about the same species composition that it has today. Non-human disturbances of fire,

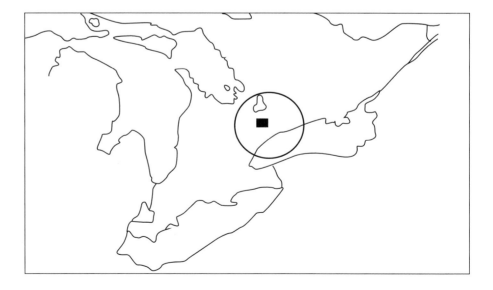

K. A. Armson

windstorms, insects and disease have changed the forest's composition, structure and ages from the very beginning, but equally, and at times more radical disturbances, have resulted from human activities.

As the ice front retreated, some seven to nine thousand years ago, an early people, the Paleo-Indians, moved in small bands into southwestern Ontario including parts of the moraine. These family units survived by hunting and fishing. Other peoples who also lived in small bands until the beginning of the first millennium A.D, and subsisted by hunting and fishing succeeded them. By 800 A.D., native peoples of the Late Woodland period had changed to an agricultural type of settlement based on crops of corn, peas and squash. This meant not only that their habitations were larger and semi-permanent, for several years in the same place, but also that these agricultural peoples cleared forest land in order to grow their crops. Continuous crop production in the same area over a period of 10 or so years would reduce the

Van Nostrand sawmill at Vandorf, late 1800s. N.B. pine sawlogs,

Photo courtesy Whitchurch-Stouffville Museum

Landsat imagery of rural area in southern Ontario showing woodlots (black lines) at back of farms. Scale:1:1,000,000.

Photo, Ontario Ministry of Natural Resources.

fertility of the sandy soils; the settlement would have to move to another forest area, clear it and begin another cycle of cultivation. The change from the early hunting and fishing way of life to agriculture resulted in population increases. Some of the Indian villages of the period, from 1000 A.D. to 1650 A.D., contained as many as 2,000 inhabitants. Since well-drained sandy soils were the easiest to clear and maintain for crop production, the forests on such areas were particularly subject to considerable human disturbance. During this period it would appear that much of the forest over significant areas, including that of the Oak Ridges Moraine, was in a relatively young successional stage of eastern white and red pines, poplars, white birch, cherries and ash—or in agricultural use by the natives. Of course there still remained significant areas of forest on wet lands, and other areas that were too difficult to clear.

K. A. Armson

By 1650 A.D. with the destruction of much of the Indian population by Iroquois from the east and south, and the withdrawal of the French, the deserted fields of the natives, including the Hurons, reverted to forest, while the already existing forests continued to grow. It is most probable that many of the large stands of eastern white pine and hardwoods that the settlers to this area saw in the early 1800s, including Bob's woodlot, became established on such lands.

The first settlements by Europeans in this area began in the 1790s largely by families following the American War of Independence and mercenary troops who had fought for the British. A 200 acre (81 hectares) lot, of which Bob's woodlot was a part, was granted by the Crown to Joseph Durham in 1803[1]. It was then sold 51 years later to Thomas Lewis (Timber Co.), then in 1869 to Dr. J. Hunter, and two years later to John Van Nostrand. All three owners had sawmills either adjacent or close to the lot and logged the forest for pine and hardwoods. In 1903, 155 acres (63 hectares) of the property were purchased by W.D. Richardson. He established a sawmill on it and cut eastern white pine, eastern white-cedar and hardwoods for farm lumber and firewood until the 1940s. In contrast to many similar properties on the Oak Ridges Moraine, Staley's property was never cleared for crops after 1803, although it has been used to pasture young cattle for several decades. Since 1803 there have been seven to eight cuts made in his woodlot, the last three, supervised by Bob using selection system silviculture. His forest still has 6,000–10,000 board feet per acre (fbm/acre) [76–127 m3/hectare] of saw timber.

The early surveys laying out the lots and concessions for settlement produced a pattern of cleared land and woodlots that can still be seen in many parts of southern Ontario. The settlers placed their buildings—houses and barns—on the road side of their lots and cleared the adjacent land usually leaving the back part of the lot in 'bush'. This is where they cut the firewood or other timbers they might use. The bush was also used as rough pasture. This resulted in an often contiguous band of woodland between each sets of farms, which produced a corridor for wildlife.

As a result of the clearing of forests for agriculture during the latter part of the 19th century and into the 20th, open fields became blow sand barrens; water erosion created large gullies and much of the area was considered wasteland. In 1922, concern

Quality trees in Staley woodlot.

Photo courtesy of Bob Staley

for remedial action resulted in counties acquiring such lands and entering into agreements with the Ontario Department of Lands and Forests to reforest and manage them. The first such area in Whitchurch–Stouffville was planted with trees in 1924 at Vivian, not far from Bob's woodlot. These plantations, mainly of red pine, have been extremely successful, and many private landowners in the area have also established plantations. As a result, erosion has been virtually eliminated on these areas and, as the forests have grown, they have produced forest products, habitats for many animal and plant species, in addition to providing recreation for local residents and, more especially, for families from the cities and towns around. The older forest lands of conifer plantations and hardwood bushes that have grown up on the old fields and wastelands during the past three-quarters of a century have so enhanced the landscape that the area is now undergoing a new form of development—mainly, but not exclusively, residential. As road access has improved and increased, enclaves of housing are now changing the landscape again and providing concern for those who see the forest landscape of the past 50 years as more environmentally desirable. What is clear is that these lands and their forests have undergone substantial change, often destructive, yet even with our knowledge of the ecological processes involved, social and economic forces will still determine what type of landscape and forests future generations will have. The principles of forest stewardship based on multiple-use values, as demonstrated in the management of the Staley woodlot, provide a useful lesson for all interested in the conservation of forest landscapes.

K. A. Armson

Northern Ontario

Bill Smith is the forest manager of approximately 200,000 hectares of forest, situated northwest of Thunder Bay, owned by a large pulp and paper company. The company has owned the freehold land and its timber resources since 1954, when it acquired the property from the Grand Trunk Pacific Railway. The forest consists of eight blocks ranging in size from 18,000 to 28,000 hectares with the first (Block 1) situated about 70 km. northwest of Thunder Bay. The remaining blocks, separated by areas of Crown forest lands, straddle the Canadian National Railways line for 280 km. from Thunder Bay to Sioux Lookout. Bill's responsibility is to manage the forest: *"To maximize long-term fibre yield to benefit Abitibi-Consolidated Inc. (the owner) and the local economy while sustaining the forest ecosystem's ability to provide a diverse set of forest values and to respond to changes in the environment."* In order to do this, forestry activities such as harvesting and renewal have to be undertaken in an ecologically sound manner, minimizing any adverse effects upon water quality and soil productivity, while maintaining or enhancing the health and diversity of all naturally occurring ecosystems and their associated plant and animal communities. Bill must also consider the protection of aesthetic features, and protect or enhance recreational opportunities for hunters, fishers, trappers, aboriginal and other forest users. As for any forest manager, a

Bill Smith standing in a 24-year-old plantation in Block 2 of the forest.

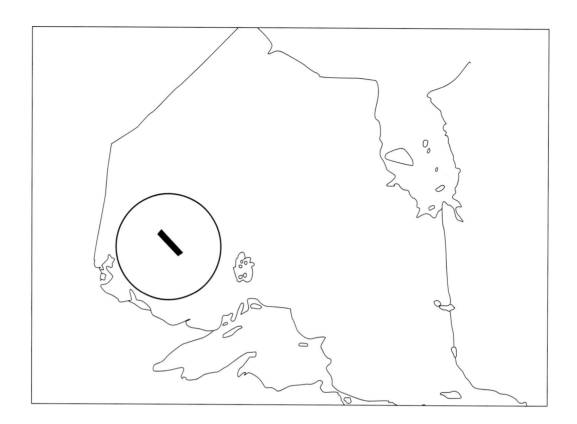

knowledge of the nature of the land base and its history is important in making day-to-day decisions, but even more so while he develops the plan for the management of the forest into the future.

The lands are primarily deep, coarse-textured sands deposited as moraines and outwash during the last retreat of the continental ice sheet about 10,000 years ago. In parts of some blocks there are areas of till deposits over bedrock. The terrain is undulating at an elevation of approximately 450 metres above sea level, with many rivers, streams and lakes in the forested landscape, which provides a wide variety of habitats; 16 per cent of the area is water.

Following the retreat of the ice, vegetation became established, passing through stages from a tundra type of open dwarf spruce and willows, to the closed forests of spruce, pine, trembling aspen, balsam poplar and white birch (i.e. those species typical of the present boreal forest). About four thousand years ago a general warming of the climate reached a peak. During this period, tree species such as eastern white and red pines, elm and

K. A. Armson

Aerial view of forest harvested
1981, seeded to jack pine 1982,
after 15 years.

Photo courtesy of Bill Smith

maple moved north from their southern ranges. With the subsequent climate cooling, the forest has returned to those species normally associated with the boreal forest; although residual eastern white and red pines (and in one block a relic stand of elm) still remain. Black spruce at 40 per cent constitutes the largest proportion of the working forest, poplar is 25 per cent, jack pine 20 per cent and balsam fir 15 per cent. These proportions have not changed from 1954 to the present, although the average age of the forest has increased from approximately 50 years in 1954 to where 50 per cent of the forest is now between 60 and 100 years old.

Throughout the millennia since the ice sheet left Ontario and until relatively recently, the forest has been subject to disturbances primarily by fire, wind, insects and diseases, with very little caused by humans. There is evidence that native peoples travelled through the area subsisting by hunting and fishing from the time of the retreat of the ice for thousands of years, but with no evidence of significant settlement. The coming of fur traders in the late 1600s and through to the early 1800s had little

Strip cutting in black spruce, 1997. N.B. revegetation of adjacent older cut areas.

Photo courtesy of Bill Smith

apparent effect on the area even though many of their travel routes did pass through parts of this forest. The opening of the Canadian west, in Manitoba particularly, resulted in events which were to bring a new set of changes. By the 1860s, there was a considerable movement of settlers from Ontario to the Red River area; the Dominion of Canada was interested in furthering development in that region as well as in what is now northwestern Ontario. To discover what possibilities existed, the government sent a series of surveyors and others to explore the lands from Thunder Bay to the Red River via Rainy River and the Lake of the Woods. In 1857, one of these persons, Simon J. Dawson, traversed by canoe and portages, a route, part of which was later developed as the Dawson Road, a portion of which traverses through Blocks Nos. 1 and 3. Dawson noted in his report[2] of the country north of Kaministikwia, *"the country seems at no distant period to have been overrun by fire,"* and later on about an area that could be in Block No.3, he notes some eastern white pine, and *"a dense growth of pitch pine* [i.e. jack pine], *spruce, tamarack, white birch and on the rising ground, poplar."* Professor H.Y. Hinds who travelled the same route that year, in his report on topographic and geological features, described the 273 miles he traversed between Kaministikwia and Fort Frances: *"The country as a whole may be regarded as a sterile waste."*

K. A. Armson

It was the construction of the Canadian Pacific Railway (CPR), however, which provided the major access through north-western Ontario, first linking Thunder Bay with Winnipeg in 1882, then Winnipeg to Montréal via Thunder Bay three years later. The CPR passes through portions of Blocks Nos. 1, 2 and 3, and there was significant logging of jack pine to provide ties as well as spruce for lumber for construction of the railway. It wasn't until much later that a major access for the remaining blocks came with the completion of the Grand Trunk Pacific Railway (now the Canadian National Railway) between Thunder Bay and Sioux Lookout in 1914. Fires following logging resulted in regeneration of jack pine and mixed poplar and conifer stands which are now harvestable. From 1930 until the acquisition of the lands in 1954, the Abitibi Power and Paper Company horse-logged the more accessible lower blocks for spruce pulpwood. Much of these areas regenerated to poplar and balsam fir rather than spruce. The balsam fir has subsequently been attacked by spruce budworm.

When Abitibi bought the land in 1954, it established a 7,000 hectare woodlands laboratory (Leo Vidlak Research Forest) in Block 3 to carry out experiments in forest regeneration (and the regeneration of black spruce, in particular). Since 1974, the forest has been available to Lakehead University for research. A comprehensive forest management plan for the 10-year period, 1995 – 2005 indicates that the capital of forest growing stock (i.e., total wood volume on the area) has increased by 29 per cent since 1954. Concurrently there has been a major diversification in the type of forest products now marketed from this forest. Current management strategies providing for sustainable forestry, for both consumptive and non-consumptive values, are in place.

Aerial view of cutover regenerated to black spruce in 1983, 11 years later. N.B. mix of tree species.

Photo courtesy of Bill Smith

Both these forests and the foresters responsible for their management exemplify how the change from simple exploitative use, mainly associated with logging for timber or as a first step in conversion to agriculture, to one of sustainable forestry, has been a relatively recent one in Ontario. Fortunately, we can still maintain forests that resemble those of past millennia. By carefully defining the values that those forests are to provide now and into the future, appropriate management strategies can be implemented. These two examples are microcosms of what is happening across much of Ontario's forest lands.

17 year-old black spruce plantation.

Photo courtesy of Bill Smith

K. A. Armson

III

Before Forests

The Bedrock Base

Much of the base of Ontario consists of bedrock that is amongst the oldest in the world. The oldest, the ancient *Precambrian* rocks, form a central belt as part of the Canadian Shield from the Québec border in the east to the northwest border with Manitoba and beyond—with a southerly extension to the upper St. Lawrence River east of Kingston. The Shield forms, in effect, the spine of Ontario. It exists as a dissected peneplain and comprises a variety of igneous, metamorphic, volcanic and sedimentary formations which have been distorted and contain a wide range of minerals. As a result of variation in structure and in mineral composition, these rocks have weathered to give rise to unconsolidated materials often quite different chemically and physically.

In southern Ontario and south of James and Hudson Bays, the Precambrian rocks are overlain by a series of sedimentary formations of Mesozoic and Paleozoic rocks laid down in ancient seas. These are predominantly sandstones, shales, and various forms of limestones. The major bedrock formations are shown in Figure 3-1. Geologically speaking, Ontario's bedrock has been modified in more recent times; in many parts of the province it still determines much of the topography and nature of the surface materials. A continental ice sheet covered all of Ontario during the last glaciation in the Pleistocene, and this did not begin to recede until some 15,000 to 20,000 years BP[1]. The ice movement, both in its advance and subsequent retreat, scoured the bedrock over which it passed while depositing materials it picked up. Glacial deposits from ice, water flowing from and within the ice sheet, and subsequent wind and water actions on them, constitute the bulk of the surface or *surficial* materials in which Ontario's soils have developed. The characteristics of the many kinds of bedrock in these transported

Figure 3-1

Major bedrock
formations of Ontario

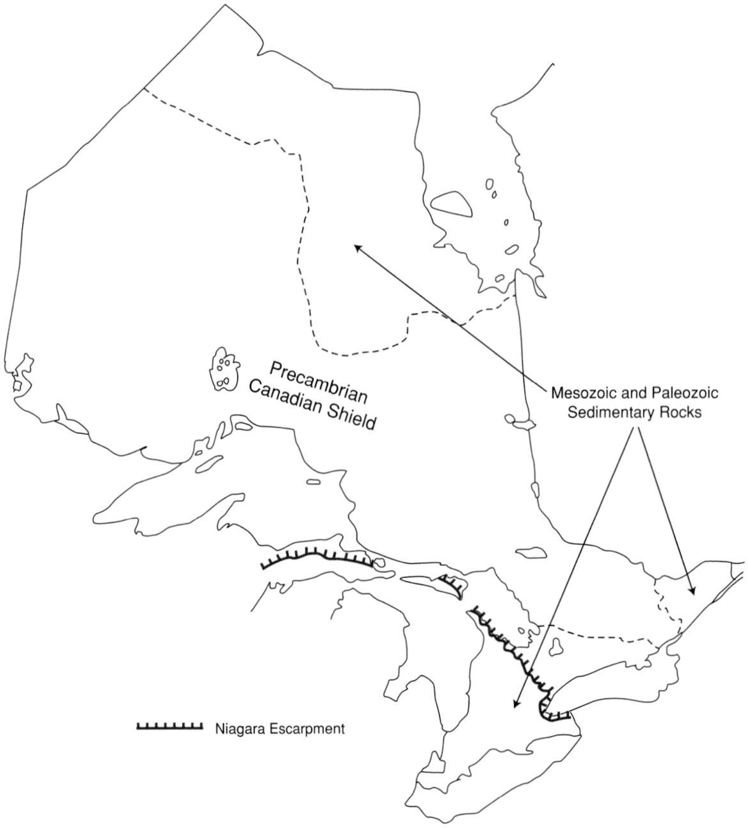

deposits, particularly their mineral and physical properties, have profoundly influenced (in conjunction with the history of vegetation on them), the nature of the soils we see today. Seldom has the soil developed directly from the *in situ* weathering of Ontario's bedrock, as is more often the case in those very old landscapes which have not been subjected to major relatively recent geologic forces, such as glaciation.

The geologic time frame is shown in Table 3-1. During the last glaciation (Pleistocene), Ontario was entirely covered by the Laurentian ice sheet which was 2–3 km thick.

The earth's surface was depressed as a result of the tremendous glacial ice mass. As the ice sheet retreated, becoming less of a burden, portions of the earth rose as an *isostatic uplift*. Such changes in elevation had a significant effect on the drainage of the waters resulting from the melting glacial ice. This determined the nature and distribution of much of the deeper surficial deposits in the province. The bedrock in many areas still provides striking topographic features as well as a variety of physical and chemical properties. In southern Ontario, the Niagara Escarpment, comprising calcareous strata of Silurian and Ordovician rocks,

K. A. Armson

extends from Niagara Falls northwesterly through to the Georgian Bay and Manitoulin Island. In the southwest, the Devonian sedimentary rocks are deeply covered by more recent surficial deposits, while in eastern Ontario, Ordovician sedimentary rocks form a relatively flat landscape. Small outcroppings of Ordovician rocks occur at the northwest end of Lake Temiskaming, and in the Algonquin and Georgian Bay regions. These are notable primarily because they are so far removed from other Ordovician formations, and occur in the midst of acidic Precambrian bedrock formations. In northwestern Ontario, Thunder Bay, and south to the Minnesota border, the topography is characterized by large meta sedimentary and meta volcanic Precambrian rocks which were part of an immense *laccolith* or dome that existed in the area of the present west end of Lake Superior. The dome has been much eroded but where harder basaltic rocks capped it, these dominate the landscape as "mountains,"—Mt. McKay, for example. The largest part of Ontario has Precambrian rock, mainly acidic, of the Canadian Shield as an underlying base for more recent deposits of varying depth. In the northwest, central and Algonquin regions, the bedrock structure defines much of the topography, and is commonly physically fractured.

The bedrocks of Ontario are physically fractured and even when they are covered by little to no mineral over burden they can support productive forests

Phanerozoic Eon

ERA	PERIOD	YEARS AGO (BP)
		– millions
Cenozoic	Quaternary *	0 – 1.6
	Tertiary	1.6 – 66.4
Mesozoic	Cretaceous	66.4 – 144
	Jurassic	144 – 208
	Triassic	208 – 245
Paleozoic	Permian	245 – 286
	Pennsylvanian	286 – 320
	Mississippian	320 – 360
	Devonian	360 – 408
	Silurian	408 – 438
	Ordovician	438 – 505
	Cambrian	505 – 570
Precambrian Eon		570 – 3700

* The Quaternary is divided into the Pleistocene (period of glaciation) and the more recent Holocene (last 10,000 years).

Table 3-1

Time scale in years from present for major geologic Eras and Periods

The Glaciation Mantle

The materials deposited by the successive glaciations of Ontario provide a mantle which modifies and superimposes on the bedrock. Although Ontario was covered by four[2] continental ice sheets during the Pleistocene Epoch of the Quaternary Period, it was the last glaciation—the Wisconsin—which provided the major deposits which constitute the province's main physiographic features, and on which much of the forests occur. As the ice sheet advanced, it picked up surface materials and gouged and scratched exposed bedrock. The materials of varying sizes—bedrock fragments, boulders, stones, sands, silts and clays—were mixed, then redeposited as the ice moved forward. This heterogeneous deposit is called *subglacial* or *basal till* and, typically, is compacted. These tills usually consist of materials and bedrock from within a relatively short distance of the ice's movement. In some locations, the ice formed hills of subglacial till called *drumlins*. These are usually smooth, oval–shaped like a whale's back, and aligned in the direction of the ice sheet's advance. Most are found in extensive areas of medium textured tills and can be quite numerous in *drumlin fields*. In these areas where surficial materials are minimal, only drumlinoidal deposits may be found; in central and northern Ontario these are usually on the north and easterly facing slopes of bedrock.

As the ice sheet was retreating, materials within the sheet were laid down, Melting water associated with the retreating ice caused some stratification of the otherwise unsorted materials; these deposits, called *supraglacial* or *ablation till*, are characteristically found on top of basal till, other material or bedrock. These deposits are loose, not compacted, often with some evidence of water-sorting.

K. A. Armson

The retreat of a glacier is not constant; there are times when the ice remains relatively stationary; it may readvance and then retreat again. When it advances more or less constantly, a glacier leaves seasonal deposits of partly stratified, coarser-textured supraglacial tills as *ground moraines* with irregular topography. When these are at the end of an advance, they are termed end or *terminal moraines*; when deposited during a progressive retreat they are *recessional moraines*. Large ice blocks left in the moraines can subsequently form small lakes or depressions. In certain places, as in southern Ontario, the ice sheet consisted of two main lobes, the Huron and Ontario-Erie lobes. During their retreat, glacial materials in the melting water flowing from the lobes formed major deposits called *interlobate moraines*. One of the best known is the Oak Ridges moraine which extends in an east-west direction from north of Toronto for approximately 160 km to the south of Campbellford. Similar large moraines occur in the north, especially in northwestern Ontario.

Waterlaid deposits, associated either directly with the melting of the ice sheet or subsequently, collectively form large areas of Ontario. Some deposits are relatively small; *kames* were formed when materials were dumped from the ice front, forming conical mounds of irregularly stratified sands and gravels. Rivers flowing both on and within the ice sheet carried loads of particles whose sizes and amounts varied with the water velocity and volume, like rivers today. When the rivers finally deposited these materials on the surface, as the ice retreated, the result was a snake-like mound of sands and gravels located in the river's final bed; these mounds are called *eskers*. Deltaic deposits of sands could often be found at the mouth of these glacial rivers where the waters emptied into lakes or seas. In central Ontario, such deposits are very extensive. As these sands were exposed in the subsequent cold dry periods, wind-blown deposits of *dunes* resulted. The area west of Kirkland Lake affords many such examples. Thin, fine, windblown deposits may also be found as a coating on supraglacial tills in ground moraines.

As the ice sheet retreated, sediments carried from it and deposited in areas subsequently exposed, gave rise to several different types of formations. Where water from rivers emptied out into lakes, deltas comprising various stratifications of sands and gravels were laid down. In other instances, where water was held in front of the ice and its materials—very finely textured silts and

The existence and relative thickness of windblown surficial deposits on tills can significantly affect a tree's root development and hence growth. Generally, the thicker the deposit the greater the growth.

clays—can be found; several such *pondings* are found in southern Ontario. A major feature of the massive amounts of water associated with melting of the ice sheet was the formation of large lakes. These *postglacial* lakes resulted in deep *lacustrine* deposits of silts and clays in northern and southern Ontario. The alternation of bands of silt and clay-sized particles is called *varves*. The cause of the alternation is the periodic difference in water flow associated with greater or lesser melting of ice. Clay deposition is the result of smaller flows, and silts result from larger flows; it is often assumed that these periodic alternations were annual. The chronology of such varves together with radiocarbon measurements have provided most of the information we have on dating these formations. When the ice readvanced over these lake deposits, the varves are often distorted or buckled.

The Chronology of Glaciation

The Pleistocene epoch lasted some 2 to 3 million years; each of the four glaciations ending with the Wisconsin is estimated to have persisted for about 100,000 years. The ice began its retreat from Ontario about 15,000 to 20,000 years BP. By about 11,000 years BP, the ice had retreated to approximately the position of a line between Sault Ste. Marie and the upper Ottawa; by 8,200 years BP, it was roughly in the area of the boundary between the Paleozoic sedimentary bedrocks in northern Ontario and the Canadian Shield (Figure 3-2).

The ice sheet was not a single "front." It existed in large lobes both in advance and retreat. The toing and froing of the ice front led to considerable complexities of depositions in some areas. As the major mass of ice melted northwards, the land mass began to rise. The sizes of post glacial lakes and the major flows of water from them were affected. These resulted in many of the topographic features we see today—such as relic shorelines for example.

The sequence of ice retreat and major postglacial lake formation is portrayed in Figures 3-3 to 3-8. [N.B. These figures are based on information from several sources, but primarily from Prest, V.K. 1970]

The ice retreat across Ontario consisted of several lobes. Two of them separated over what is now southwestern Ontario and gave rise to a series of moraines. Melting waters formed Lake Maumee which drained south into the valley of the Mississippi. The exposed land mass between Lake Maumee and the ice front of the lobes has been called the "Ontario Island" (Figure 3-3). In later stages, Lake Maumee was succeeded by Lakes Arkona, Whittlesey and Warren. Over the next two thousand years or so, the ice front retreated in a general northeasterly direction. Access to the exposed

Figure 3-2

Approximate position of ice front Years BP

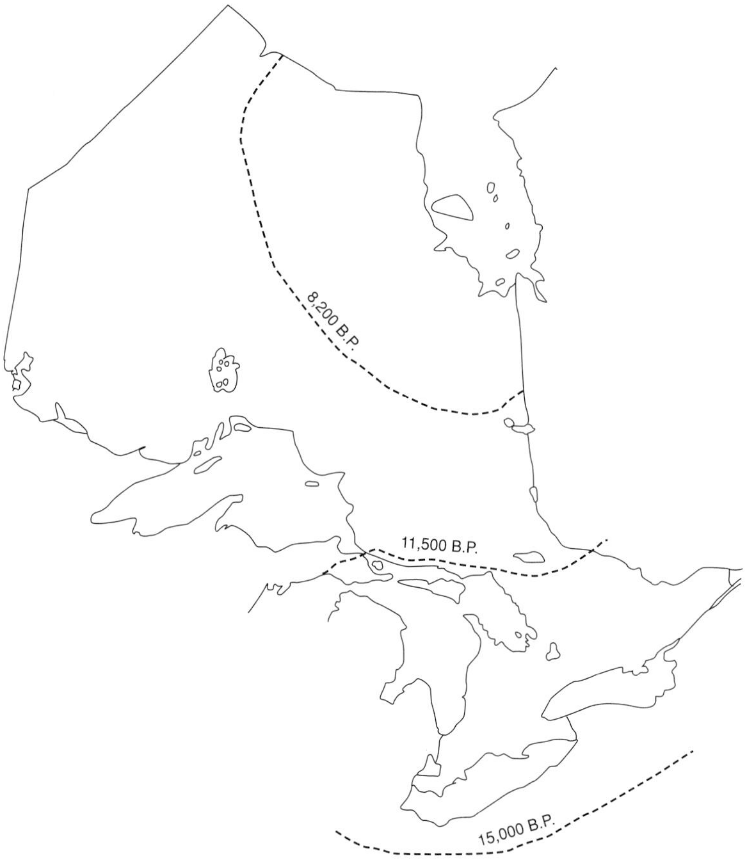

lands of southern Ontario was from either the Michigan or New York locations and large post glacial lakes, created from the melting ice began to take the form of the present Great Lakes system. (Figure 3-4.)

During this same period Lake Agassiz, which covered part of northwestern Ontario, was formed. As the ice retreated from the valley of the St. Lawrence, the land remained depressed, and sea water moved into the upper St. Lawrence and Ottawa valleys. It would be called the Champlain Sea (Figure 3-5). Lake Algonquin was at its highest level at this time.

A major change in the drainage of Lake Algonquin occurred with the opening of an outlet through North Bay—the Fossmill outlet—into the Champlain Sea. The level of the lake fell and Algonquin was succeeded by two lakes—Hough and Stanley. Lake Minong, a precursor to the present Lake Superior and Lake Barlow in the northeast also appeared. (Figure 3-6.) A further melting resulted in Lake Barlow-Ojibway whose sediments form the basis

K. A. Armson

for much of the materials in the Clay Belt. When the ice front was roughly at the northern boundary of the Precambrian with Mesozoic and Paleozoic sediments (Hudson Bay lowlands), it made a series of readvances over the lacustrine deposits of much of Lake Barlow-Ojibway, which resulted in redeposition of till and "shoving" of the lacustrine varves.

At the time of the Cochrane Advance, the sea began entering from the north and, with the final retreat of the ice from Ontario, occupied much of the James Bay lowlands as the Tyrrell Sea.

Figure 3-3
The uncovering of the "Ontario island"
and Lake Maumee.
14ka BP [ka = 1,000 years]

Figure 3-4
Retreat of the ice to central Ontario
and the main post glacial lakes.
12–12.5ka BP

Figure 3-5
Lakes Agassiz, Algonquin and the Champlain Sea.
11.8–10.6ka BP

Figure 3-6
Lakes Barlow, Minong, Hough and Stanley.
10.6–9.5ka BP

Figure 3-7
Lakes Houghton-Nipissing and Stanley-
Nipissing, and the Cochrane Advance.
9.5–8.1ka BP

Figure 3-8
Final retreat of ice from Ontario and Tyrrell
Sea. 8.1–7.5ka B.P.

K. A. Armson

The Physiography of Ontario

The physiography of an area consists of two elements: its topography or surface features (such as shape and slope), and the nature of the materials which form the "body" of that surface. Together with aspect and drainage, the description of any physiographic component constitutes what is often referred to as a *site description* at the local or ground level. For example, a site might be described as, "a northeast-facing slope of 7–8° with irregular surface on a deep (30 cm +), well-drained ablation till of stony sandy loam." Topography, aspect and drainage are important because all of them modify the local climatic factors of temperature and exposure, and can have a determining effect on species distribution. Generally, for most purposes, especially those related to land or resource management, it is customary to consider physiographic features at relatively large scales, e.g. 1:10,000–1:20,000. If the province of Ontario (with its maximum east-west and north-south distances each of approximately 1,690 km) was represented by a map on a page 21 x 21 cm, the scale of representation would be about 1:8,000,000. What can be portrayed at such a scale is much less than when larger scales such as 1:500,000 or 1:20,000 are used.

An understanding of the importance of scale is essential both when we portray information about land resources and forests, and when we develop relationships between specific site features on the ground and their application and extrapolation to other areas. Often individual features mapped at ground level show patterns that would otherwise be overlooked unless collectively portrayed at a much smaller scale. For example, individual drumlins may be identified in the field (large scale) but when they are mapped at a smaller scale it becomes apparent that they occur in "fields" and have the same orientation.

Figure 3-9 shows a generalized view of the main physiographic formations in Ontario in terms of their materials. Lacustrine and deltaic deposits (clays, silts and sands) are usually level to undulating unless there has been subsequent reworking by ice, water or wind. Areas of tills and clay tills more typically reveal a rolling topography. Large areas, mostly those of the Precambrian shield with relatively shallow deposits, have a highly variable topography determined by the nature of their bedrock components. In many areas of the shield, the topography is rough with sharp changes in slope and aspect, providing a great variety of physical sites for tree growth and other organisms. Ontario is not a land of elevation extremes; it ranges from sea level at the Hudson and James Bays to a maximum of about 650 metres in the northwestern area of the province.

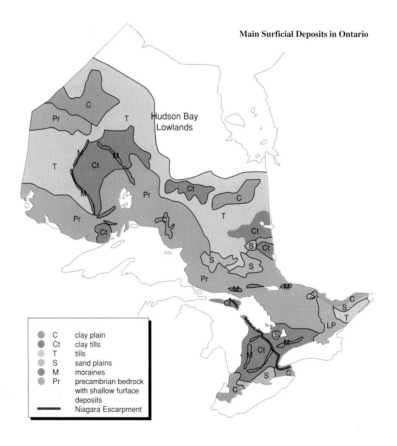

Figure 3-9 Main Surficial Deposits in Ontario

(Based on Chapman and Putnam, 1966, and Sado and Carswell, 1987)

K. A. Armson

The moraine areas in southwestern Ontario border the "Ontario Island" which emerged during the retreat of the two ice lobes—Huron and the Ontario-Erie lobes as depicted in Figure 3-3. Deep deltaic deposits of sands and silts into glacial lakes Whittlesey and Warren form the large sand plain that covers much of Norfolk County and extends north to Brantford. A series of clay plains in the extreme southwest, characterized by gentle topography and limited drainage in many parts, is the result of sediment from Lakes Whittlesey and Warren. A series of large moraines occur in northwestern Ontario mainly west of Lake Nipigon. Relatively flat areas of clay and silts from lakes Agassiz and Barlow-Ojibway are extensive and, as we noted earlier have been modified by the Cochrane readvance in the northeast. In central Ontario, there are large areas of deep open (> 2m) sand deposits originating from large rivers flowing from the ice front and forming deltas in the lakes into which they flowed. Most of the materials deposited in southern Ontario are calcareous, reflecting the sedimentary bedrocks over which the ice passed. This is also true for materials in portions of Ontario's northland where deposits originated from calcareous bedrocks in the region. The soils in both areas have had calcium leached to lower levels as a result of the establishment of vegetation, and the weathering of calcareous materials over time. Most of the areas in central and southern northwest Ontario are acidic and comprise materials from the Precambrian rocks over which the ice passed. The fractured Precambrian, Silurian and Ordovician bedrocks, without or with very shallow (< 20 cm) surficial materials support quite productive forests, in part because of adaptive root types of several tree species such as pines and certain deciduous trees.

Surface elevations for Ontario are shown in Figure 3-10. Mostly, they reflect the surfaces of the underlying bedrock formations, with some modifications from more recent surficial deposit. For example, the high elevation of southwestern Ontario's "Ontario Island" resulted from sequential moraine deposits during advances and retreats of the ice during glaciation.

Figure 3-10
Elevations in Ontario.

(Adapted from Mackey, B.G. et al. 1994. A new digital elevation model for Ontario.) Can. Forest Service, Ontario. ON.NODA/NFP Tech Rep. TR-6. 26p. + appendix

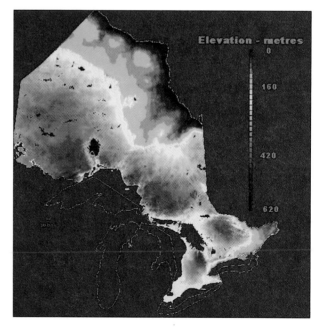

The Climate of Ontario

The climate of Ontario during the retreat of the Laurentian ice sheet, and to the time of first direct records, can be deduced from observations of current conditions and their related climates. Then by using evidence of similar conditions occurring in the past, one can infer similar climates. For Ontario,[3] forest tree species have been the major source of such evidence. Current pollen profiles, compiled by species, were compared to the existing forest composition to create a correlation base. Then radiocarbon-dated samples from a series of locations across the province were profiled, making it possible to reconstruct climates based on the forest compositions of earlier periods. Weather conditions immediately preceding the ice were arctic-like. As the ice retreated, the climate warmed. Postglacial lakes exercised a moderating climatic influence, just as the existing Great Lakes do now. By 8,000 BP, the climate in southern Ontario was similar to that which exists today. In northern Ontario a modern temperature was reached later, by 6,500 BP; however, this was then followed by a millennium (6,500–5,500 BP) of a much warmer climate, sometimes referred to as the *Hypsithermal* period.

Ontario lies between Latitude 42° N and 56° N, and Longitude 74° 30 and 94°. This means that the province is exposed to a wide range of climatic and weather conditions. The main weather systems are from the Arctic, the Pacific and to a lesser degree the Atlantic, plus tropical air masses originating in the south. Prevailing winds are westerly, northwest, west and southwest and, much less frequently, from the northeast and southeast. The Great Lakes influence the climate by moderating temperatures and by adding atmospheric moisture, particularly in those areas in the lee of the

K. A. Armson

lakes. The average annual total precipitation ranges between 50 to 100 cm. Snowfall generally contributes one third or less of the total precipitation, with two exceptions. In the extreme southwest, although variable from year to year, snowfall rarely constitutes more than a quarter of the total precipitation and does not remain for more than a few days at a time. In the lee of the Great Lakes, one half of the precipitation can be as snowfall and it may remain on the ground for periods of three to four months. Figure 3-11 shows the patterns of mean annual precipitation for the province.

The two areas of highest precipitation (100 cm) are in the lee of Georgian Bay and Lake Huron. For most of the forest areas, the average annual total precipitation is 60 to 85 cm.

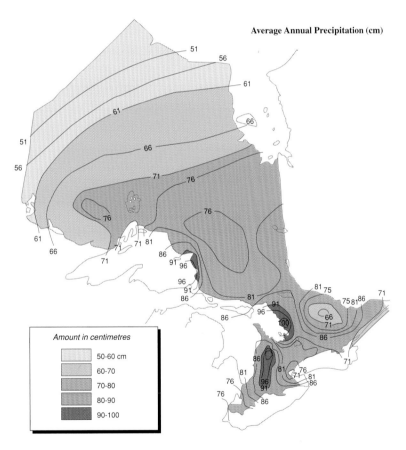

Figure 3-11

Pattern of average annual precipitation in Ontario. (Based on Brown et al, 1968 and Chapman and Thomas, 1968)

As important, if not more important than total precipitation, is the availability of water for plants' use during the growing season. Local factors of topography, soil, and aspect play a major role, but it is the balance between the total precipitation available and that required for *evapotranspiration* that is most important on a regional basis. Using Thornthwaite's determinations for evapotranspiration, water deficiency is low throughout northern and southern Ontario where it is 2 to 5 cm, although over a full year there is, in fact, a water surplus. There is little documented research information on water use and possible deficits for specific forest areas, with the exception of a study of a central Ontario forest of mixed conifers and hardwoods in the Great Lakes – St. Lawrence region on shallow, stony, silty, sand till over Precambrian granite-gneiss bedrock. That forest is typical of many tens of thousands of hectares of such forest in the province, and it was determined[4] that it had an annual average moisture deficit of 5.7 cm, with large monthly variation during any year, but that the year to year variation was not significant.

As might be expected, there is considerable variation in average annual frost-free periods for the province, ranging from 180 days in the extreme southwest to less than half that (70–80 days) in northern Ontario. Two other factors influence the length of frost-free periods. One is elevation, with lower values as elevation increases. (90 average annual frost-free days occur in the Algonquin

Figure 3-12
Sugar maple bush damaged by 1998 ice storm

(photo by Mike Rosen)

K. A. Armson

uplands and the highest locations in northern Ontario for example, at least 20 days less than at lower elevations.) The second factor concerns location along the Great Lakes, where an increase of 20 days over locations several kilometres inland can be expected.

Thunderstorms and severe windstorms are other factors which affect Ontario's forests—the former by causing forest fires, and the latter by blowing down trees.

Thunderstorms are less frequent in northern than in southern Ontario, but their effects on forests are greatest in the north. Northwestern Ontario, particularly in the Rainy River-Kenora area, experiences a higher number of storms than in the rest of the north and, as one might expect, the northwest has the largest forest areas of fire-origin.

The blowdown of large forest areas places a great amount of combustible organic debris on the forest floor, and this, if ignited by lightening or human cause, can deplete a forest much more seriously than a fire that occurs in a standing forest. Windstorms during the frost-free period are responsible for the blowdown of individual trees that are either dead or unhealthy. The root systems of felled trees bring up mineral soil which acts as a type of cultivation. Thus not only is there an opening in the tree canopy as a tree falls over but the exposed mineral soil also provides a seed bed which many tree and other plant species will use. A severe forest fire leaves many dead standing trees (*chicots*) and large contiguous areas may show the effects of such wind throws. Although ice storms are not rare, they have usually been minor factors in affecting tree growth. In January 1998, however, a major ice storm in eastern Ontario and Québec caused major destruction and mortality—particularly in deciduous forests.

In summary the geology and geological forces of the past created the physiographic landscape on which Ontario's forests have developed over the past 10,000 years and more. Locally, climatic forces of wind, water and more infrequently ice, together with wildfires, have provided the disturbances that formed particular forests at any given time. These disturbances are still ongoing, sometimes modified by human actions such as fire suppression or, to a greater extent, by human exploitation and management.

Tree species such as jack pine and black spruce are adapted to fire and will regenerate naturally after a major forest fire

IV

Greening Up

The forebears for most of the tree species in Ontario's forests date back many millions of years to the early Tertiary or late Cretaceous periods (Table 3-1). Several of the most common conifers—white and black spruce and jack pine—are considered to be relatively young species originating perhaps only a million or so years ago. Whatever the earlier history, the documentation that is particularly relevant to understanding today's forests is that dating from the period of the last glaciation, the Wisconsin, and subsequently the past 15 to 20 thousand years. When the last ice sheet was at its fullest extent, trees and other plant species south of the glacier were found either in geographically limited areas or widely distributed latitudinally. In limited areas these trees could be found in the Appalachians, the eastern coastal region, or in the south in the Gulf coastal plain. They were widespread, especially latitudinally, from the Atlantic coast in the east across through the middle of the continent. Thus eastern white pine spread north from an area in Virginia, while white spruce and black spruce, which were present in a wide band from the east across to the midwest, are considered to have moved north in a two-pronged fashion, from the east entering southern Ontario and from the west into Manitoba and northwestern Ontario. The main boreal species of poplar, birch, balsam fir, tamarack, and spruce are widely distributed now and were equally so in a broad band in front of the main continental ice fronts.

Figure 4-1, based on pollen analyses, illustrates the time frames for the movement of a number of major tree species into southern Ontario.

The initial vegetation which grew up in front of the ice, as the ice retreated, was treeless; dwarf shrubs and species of tundra-type plants colonized the recently exposed mineral soil. This growth was succeeded by spruce, first in open-grown and then in closed forests, reaching a maximum in southwestern Ontario around 11,500 years BP. This was also the period when mastodons and mammoths were found in Ontario's forests. The spruces gradually moved into northern Ontario, probably from two components. Southern migration originated in southern Ontario and spread progressively north as the ice front retreated. A second migration originated in the midwest and moved into Manitoba and north-western Ontario. By 4,000 years BP, there was an extensive spruce forest in the north. Although we do not yet have any firm evidence, it has been assumed that white spruce occupied the better drained sites and black spruce the wetter areas. Red spruce, in contrast with white and black spruce, migrated from fragmented popula-tions within the Appalachians. Little is known of its history of movement through eastern Ontario westerly into the south-central parts of the province where it now exists in fragmented stands or in mixtures with other species.

The second group of conifers to move into Ontario was the pines. At the time of the maximum southern limit of the Wisconsin glaciation, red and jack pine and the southern hard pines were to be found in the unglaciated regions of the Atlantic coastal plain, the central and eastern Gulf coastal plain and the north half of Florida. Red and jack pine moved north into southern Ontario about 11,000 years BP following the spruces, where they reached their maximum extent about 10,000 years ago. Hard on their heels,

Figure 4-1

Generalized tree pollen diagram for southern Ontario.

(adapted from Karrow and Warner, 1990)

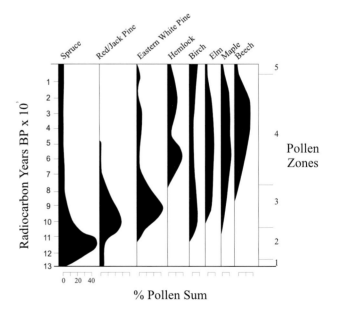

K. A. Armson

came the eastern white pine which achieved its maximum a millennium later, although it remains a more consistent and larger component up to the present. At the time of Lakes Hough and Stanley (Figure 3-6), spruce dominated areas like Manitoulin Island, while eastern white pine was increasing on the mainland. Eastern white pine moved from areas in the Appalachians to the north and west, reaching its most northern abundance in Ontario about 5,000 years BP at the time of the hypsithermal maximum, when temperatures were warmer than today. Eastern white pine populations extended farther north in abundance than they do today, although relic individuals and small stands still exist in present-day northern Ontario. Figure 4-2 shows the sequential abundance of eastern white pine from 12,000 years BP to the present, based on fossil pollen data. Interestingly the pollen diagram for eastern white pine in southern Ontario (Figure 4-1) also shows an increase at that same period. Another increase about 400–500 years BP will be discussed in Chapter V.

Balsam fir, one of the conifer species which was spread widely across the continent from the Atlantic coast to the interior, moved north, although not as rapidly as the spruces and pines. At 12,000 years BP when southwestern Ontario was free of ice and the front was north of Lake Simcoe (Figure 3-4), balsam fir was extending from two centres: the western one in Iowa, and an eastern one which moved into southern Ontario and then north. The western centre moved into Manitoba and northwestern Ontario and, by about 6,000 years BP, was north of latitude 55° N east of Hudson Bay, although it remained at a lower latitude in the west. During the warmer period (ca. 4,000 years BP), balsam fir is estimated to have comprised 20 to 30 per cent of the forest in central Ontario east of Lake Superior.

The movement of tamarack (or larch) is interesting because at 20,000 years BP, this species is believed to have occurred in a single refugium in Tennessee. By 8,000 years BP, it occupied much of the deglaciated area to the north and west, being limited in the latter only by prairie. As today, tamarack was usually found in bogs and swamps, although undoubtedly, it would grow well on upland soils when there was adequate moisture—as it does now. Tamarack, and white and black spruce are the conifers whose ranges extend into the northern tundra around Hudson and James Bays.

Like the tamarack, the eastern hemlock of 20,000 years BP occurred in a single refugium in Tennessee. It moved north through

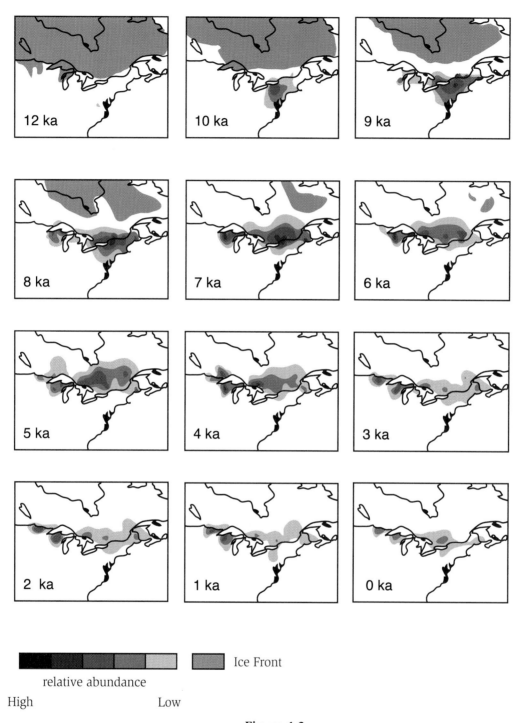

Figure 4-2

Relative abundance of eastern white pine during the past 12,000 years based on fossil pollen data

(from Jacobson Jr. and Dieffenbacher-Krall, 1995)

K. A. Armson

the Appalachians and followed eastern white pine into Ontario reaching a peak in southern Ontario about 6,000 to 7,000 years ago. In Ontario's Muskoka area, as elsewhere, hemlock declined rapidly over a relatively short period at about 4,900 years BP with a subsequent increase over the next couple of millennia.

Eastern redcedar (juniper) and eastern white-cedar separated from the southern species of their respective genera (Juniperus and Thuya) at about the same time, 20,000 years BP, that red and jack pine were separating from their southern pine species. While both cedars spread north, the eastern redcedar was much more restricted in its range than eastern white-cedar which spread north to the Hudson Bay-James Bay lowlands. There is evidence that eastern white-cedar expanded north particularly during 6,000 to 4,000 years BP when the climate was much warmer.

Species of birch existed during the last glaciation in two eastern centres—the east coast and Louisiana. A third centre was in the midwest but by the time this population began to spread north into deglaciated areas, it apparently coalesced with its migrant neighbours. Birch spread into northwestern Ontario from the midwest, while in the southern and northeastern parts of Ontario and general areas of eastern Canada, birches spread from the east. In Ontario, the abundance of birch was high 7,000 years BP, declining somewhat by 6,000 years BP. Generally, as now, birch increases in abundance from south to north.

The main location of poplars during glaciation was in the south, from Missouri to Alabama and the Gulf coastal plain. As they moved north, the population separated into two centres, one on the east (Ohio and western New York), the other in Minnesota and Wisconsin. Poplars rapidly spread as the ice retreated and, by the time of the Champlain Sea (Figures 3-5 and 3-6), poplars were estimated to comprise 60 to 80 per cent of the forest on the sea's south and southwest borders.

Ash, particularly black ash, was one of the earliest deciduous trees to colonize deglaciated wet soils. Ash was widespread from the Atlantic coast to the continental midwest prior to the retreat of the Laurentian ice sheet. It moved into southern Ontario areas bordering the retreating ice from 12,000 to 10,000 years BP. By 4,000 years BP, it was widespread, extending from the Gulf of the St. Lawrence across to latitude 55° N, west of Hudson Bay.

Elms spread in a similar fashion; widespread from east to the midwest they moved north to occupy much the same range as ash

Some of Ontario's tallest trees

Pine

(Eastern white pine—
Pinus strobus)
Located in Haliburton County, this tree has a diameter of 172 centimetres with a height of 45.1 metres

Red Pine

(Pinus resinosa)
Located in Algonquin Park, this tree has a diameter of 113 centimetres with a height of 37.5 metres.

White Spruce

(Picea glauca)
Located in McClure Township, Hastings County, this tree has a diameter of 79 centimetres with a height of 39 metres.

The Mystery of the Killing of the Hemlock Trees

The reconstruction of what ancient forests were like is a type of sleuthing somewhat similar to that done by detectives in their attempts to determine "who did it?", only the time-frame is much greater—millennia, rather than days, months or a few years. The measurement of fossil pollen from lake bed sediments is a prime source of information, particularly when it can be "benchmarked" against a known population and radio-carbon dated. Normally, the changes in tree species occur relatively gradually and in relation to known or rationally inferred causes. When there is an apparent rapid decline in the presence of a single species, not in other species and for no apparent reason, the hunt is on.

Such is the case with the sudden reduction in the pollen of eastern hemlock about 4,900 years BP. Since this was also during a period of somewhat warmer climate, that might be superficially assumed to be the cause, but that would be wrong. Consider that:

1. the decline occurred at the same time throughout the known and wide range of eastern hemlock;
2. the decline occurred over a wide range of soil and climatic conditions that are known to affect hemlock growth and regeneration;
3. following the decline there was an increase in the successional tree species such as birch and subsequently maple, beech, oak and white pine in the same areas, and
4. the decline occurred over a very short time, estimated by some as little as 50 years.

Both insect and disease organisms can bring about a widespread mortality of an organism, especially if the causal agents are introduced and not indigenous to the area of the host species. One postulation has been that the western hemlock looper became introduced to the east and ravaged the eastern hemlock which had no resistance to it. A second scenario proposes that a pathogen was the cause and that over several hundreds or a thousand or so years the surviving hemlock were those that had a resistance and these formed the basis for the species resurgence. It did not come back to pre-decline levels until some 1,900 years later. The only other North American species for which there are recorded data of an analogous decline is the killing of the American chestnut (Castanea dentata). It was the victim of the introduced blight (Cryphonectria parasitica) between 1904, when the disease was found in New York, and the 1950s. The patterns of decline for both tree species when compared were similar. What is different is that the hemlock is again a common species, and chestnut is not. Although perhaps we should wait a thousand or so more years!

K. A. Armson

by 6,000 years BP. Even today, the range of white or American elm is one of the widest, in latitude and climatic conditions, extending from Florida and the Gulf Coast to the Arctic height of land in northern Ontario—a range exceeded only by red maple.

At the time of maximum glaciation, maple occurred in a wide area from the southern Appalachians south to the Gulf Coast and west as far as Kansas. It spread into southern Ontario about 10,500 years BP and became abundant by 6,000 years BP, and remains a significant component of the forests in the Great Lakes – St. Lawrence region to the present. The increase in maple was coincident with the decrease in eastern white pine in the same areas (Figure 4-1).

All the genera mentioned so far, whether conifers or broad-leaved trees, have seeds which are winged and capable of dispersal by wind, as well as other means.

American beech and oaks have nut seeds. These either germinate where they fall or are moved by animals such as squirrels. The American beech range was smaller than that of the oak prior to deglaciation—limited as it was to the eastern and south Gulf coastal plain and north Florida. Oaks enjoyed a broader latitudinal range. Surprisingly, both American beech and oaks moved rather rapidly north from their glacial retreats. Both were in southern Ontario by 8,000 years BP and oaks extended west to the shores of Lake Agassiz (Figure 3-5).

Basswood, as far as is known, spread north from a single refugium in south central Alabama. It is associated with fertile soils and by 6,000 to 4,000 years BP was relatively abundant but with a restricted latitudinal range. It had two population centres, one in southeastern Ontario and New York, the other in southern Wisconsin. By 2,000 years BP, basswood was not a major species in Ontario's forests.

Walnut, including butternut, spread like the basswood from only one known site (20,000 years BP) in north central Louisiana, arriving in southern Ontario by 6,000 years BP. Hickories came into southern Ontario by 8,000 years BP, but have existed only as a fragmented population. Although both walnut and hickory pollens are recorded in the Lake Nipissing area along with fossil pollen of sycamore (which is far north of its present limit in southwestern Ontario), it is most likely that their presence does not reflect a local population but anomalies carried long distances by air currents from the south.

*O*ntario's Forest Regions

Three of Canada's forest regions are in Ontario (Figure 4-3). The southernmost, the *Deciduous Region* is unique in Canada. The *Boreal* forest occupies northern Ontario and the *Great Lakes – St. Lawrence Region* ranges throughout the middle areas of the province from the southeast to the northwest.

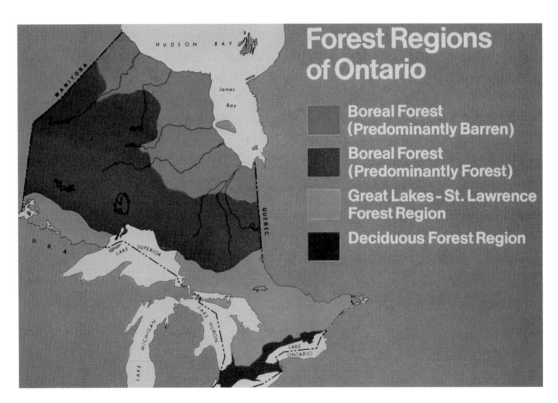

Figure 4-3 The Forest Regions of Ontario

K. A. Armson

Figure 4-4
Aerial view of the boreal forest in
northwestern Ontario

The Boreal region has a northern component, the Boreal Barrens, which is a subarctic open lichen woodlands wherein black, and to a lesser degree, white spruce and tamarack are the main tree species together with willow. The main conifer species of the Boreal region are black and white spruce, jack pine, balsam fir, tamarack and eastern white-cedar, with the spruces and jack pine being most abundant. Tamarack and eastern white-cedar are generally found on the wetter soils. The predominant deciduous hardwood species are two poplars—trembling aspen and balsam poplar—and white birch. Shrubs and small trees of willow, alder and other genera also comprise major components of the Boreal.

The Great Lakes – St. Lawrence region has a wide range of tree species, including many of those found in the Boreal region. Red and eastern white pine, eastern hemlock, balsam fir, eastern white-cedar, sugar maple, white and yellow birch, red oak and basswood are characteristic. There are also a number of other trees and shrubs such as ironwood, striped and mountain maple, the cherries (red, black and choke), serviceberry and elderberry, which, together with a rich herbaceous vegetation, make this region one of the most floristically varied in Canada. This variation is a reflection of the differences in bedrock geology and physiography of the region. For example, on the shallow limestone plains adjacent to the Precambrian shield, an open type of vegetation flourishes along with scattered trees. This vegetation is maintained by a combination of drought and periodic fires, in a condition termed an *alvar*.

In Canada the Deciduous region is exclusive to southern Ontario. It contains virtually all of the main tree species in the Great Lakes–St. Lawrence region. In addition, particularly in the south, there exist broadleaved trees commonly found in Ohio, Pennsylvania, Virginia and the Carolinas: black walnut, butternut, magnolia, black gum, tulip, several oaks (black, pin, chinquapin), hickories, sassafras, red bud and eastern flowering dogwood.

The Deciduous also contains species found in the southern part of the Great Lakes – St. Lawrence region: butternut and eastern redcedar depending on soil and other habitat factors.

Each of these regions has been subdivided into sections which reflect differences in vegetation related primarily to physiography and local climate. One feature of southern Ontario at the time of European settlement was the occurrence of tallgrass prairie and savannah, particularly in the extreme southwest north of Lake Erie. Presently, there are somewhat more than two thousand hectares of this landscape in southwestern Ontario, mainly on well-drained sands. Associated tree species are oaks—black, pin and white— together with eastern white pine. Such species were, undoubtedly, maintained by relatively frequent fires. These trees have been the

Conifer family

Figure 4-5

A Great Lakes – St. Lawrence broadleaved forest in the Fall. Photo courtesy Peter Hynard

K. A. Armson

subject of intensive studies, in a concerted effort to maintain and restore the flora and fauna of tallgrass and savannahs in south-western Ontario[1].

Observations of prairie and savannahs by Europeans in the 1800s were relatively common, in part because these were the open areas attractive to settlers. These landscapes undoubtedly resulted from a combination of conditions. Wetland prairies would occur where rivers meandered and were subject to seasonal flooding, but frequent fires often set by Aboriginals during dry periods both on these areas and on uplands would maintain the prairie and savannah conditions. Openness and proximity to water of Ontario's prairie and savannah areas meant they often became the site of settlers' establishments and towns.

Broadleaf family

The northern movement of tree species during the hypsithermal period meant that the ecotone or transition zone between the Boreal and Great Lakes – St. Lawrence regions also moved north. Areas in central Ontario, now in the Boreal region, were in forests similar to those of the Great Lakes–St. Lawrence region between 7,000 to 3,000 years BP. Since then, subsequent climate cooling has resulted in a reversion of these areas to Boreal forest conditions, and the replacement of eastern white pine by spruce, jack pine and balsam fir.

Figure 4-6
Flowering dogwoods in the Deciduous forest region

Broadleaved Age Classes - All Ownerships

Areas of Intolerant & Tolerant Forests in thousands of hectares
Intolerant (poplars, birches etc.); Tolerant (maples, beech etc.)

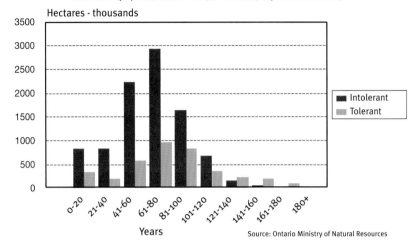

Source: Ontario Ministry of Natural Resources

Boreal Forest Region

Main Species' Working Groups
Areas as Percent of Total WG's

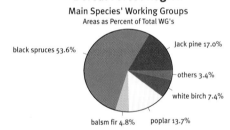

Source: Ontario Ministry of Natural Resources

Great-Lakes-St. Lawrence & Deciduous Forest Regions

Main Species' Working Groups
Areas as Percent of Total WG's

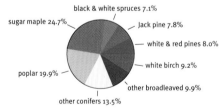

Source: Ontario Ministry of Natural Resources

A Working Group consists of the aggregate of all stands having the same predominant species and managed under a similar silvicultural system.

K. A. Armson

The Trees

Conifers

Spruces _____

Three of the five native spruce trees to Canada occur in Ontario. Both white and black spruce are widespread and have similar ranges in Ontario and Canada. Red spruce is predominantly a species of the maritime provinces and is found only in scattered stands in southcentral Ontario. White spruce will grow on a wide range of soils but, unlike black spruce, is not found on deep organic soils such as peats. White spruce is common in both the Boreal and Great Lakes – St. Lawrence regions, growing in mixed wood stands with birch, poplars and balsam fir. Most of the northern forests have a fire origin; the season in which fires occur, their nature, magnitude, frequency, intensity and duration can significantly influence the type and amount of regeneration of each forest species. Intervals between major seed crops of white spruce range from 2–6 years; the cones mature in one year, opening with seed dispersal in late August and September. Thus severe crown fires at any time are likely to result in minimal white spruce regeneration, whereas a ground fire in mid to late summer in stands where white spruce is carrying a mid to heavy cone crop would most likely create conditions (by removing surface organic material) that provide a favourable seedbed for white spruce regeneration.

In contrast, black spruce, while having a similar frequency in terms of major seed crops, differs in that the cones remain partially closed on the trees, and the seeds are dispersed over several years. Black spruce is adapted to regenerate under a wide range of fire conditions even after severe crown fires. When the lowermost

White Spruce

Inventoried Forest Lands—Age Classes

Areas of Conifer (Softwood) Forest by Age Classes
Areas in thousands ('000's) of hectares

Age Class 20 yr. classes	Ontario Crown			Federal	Private	Total
	Parks & Reserves	Other	Total			
0–20	266.6	3593.8	3860.4	18.6	469.9	4348.9
21–40	132.5	1422.4	1554.9	8.7	147.3	1710.9
41–60	434.0	2747.0	3181.0	30.2	378.6	3589.8
61–80	553.3	3729.0	4282.3	58.4	477.4	4818.1
81–100	476.4	3266.1	3742.5	59.1	253.4	4055.0
101–120	394.9	2542.4	2937.3	23.7	105.9	3066.9
121–140	385.9	2123.0	2508.9	10.6	77.6	2597.1
141–160	414.1	1492.7	1906.8	8.7	42.7	1958.2
161–180	72.5	275.3	347.8	1.1	6.6	355.5
180+	15.5	47.7	63.2	0.3	1.5	65.0

Gross Total Volumes—millions of cubic metres

Conifer	382.9	2832.0	3214.9	33.4	248.2	3496.5

Mean Annual Increment—thousands of cubic metres per year

Conifer	4483.3	33783.6	38266.9	416.7	3574.1	42257.7

Conifer (Softwood) Age Classes by Ownership

Areas in thousands of hectares

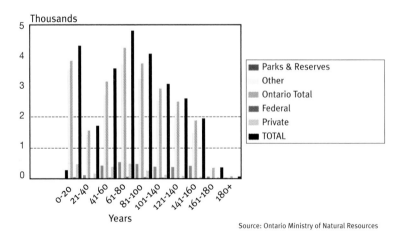

Source: Ontario Ministry of Natural Resources

K. A. Armson

branches of black spruce are in contact with the uppermost organic layers of the soil, especially in peat soils, the branches may develop roots and vegetatively produce new trees termed *layerings*.

White spruce shows considerable genetic variation with differences in crown form, time of bud opening and growth. It has a flexible root system which can exploit deep soils and unconsolidated materials, whereas black spruce consistently has a shallow, widespread lateral root system located mainly in the upper 20–30 cm, no matter how deep the soil may be. Although there is clinal genetic variation from south to north, no differences relating to whether seedlings originate from upland or lowland sites have been recorded. Black spruce has a very consistent narrow crown form in sharp contrast to the wider spreading crown of white spruce.

Black Spruce

Figure 4-7
Black spruce showing narrow conical crowns, upper part "pruned" by squirrels

Figure 4-8
Jack pine stand in northwestern Ontario Photo by Brian Nicks

Jack Pine

Red Pine

Pines

Although there are four pines native to Ontario, one of them, pitch pine, occurs only in a very limited area in the southeastern part of the province close to the St. Lawrence. It is a curiosity that pitch pine can withstand major injury from fire or browsing by producing new growth from dormant buds.

Jack pine is the most abundant pine, occurring throughout the Boreal region over a wide range of soils and drainage conditions, although it is primarily associated with well-drained coarser-textured soils, or shallow soils over fractured bedrock following forest fires. Like black spruce, jack pine has serotinous cones which remain on the tree for several years, releasing their seeds when the bonding of the cone scales is broken as a result of heat from forest fires. Jack pine shows considerable genetic variation and this is reflected by differences in form and growth. The root system is flexible and can develop vertically where suitable soil conditions exist.

Red pine is unusual in two respects. First, it is a species that shows virtually no genetic variation. Second, for many years it was the most commonly planted tree in southern Ontario, particularly on abandoned farm lands on sandy soils. It was the main species used for reforestation from the 1920s to the 1950s. Its root system is deep-going and limited primarily by physical obstruction or, in coarser-textured soils by the presence of calcium carbonate. While its cones are not serotinous, the species does regenerate, especially when a hot summer ground fire occurs prior to a major seed crop. Red pine is intolerant of shade and grows best in the open. Natural red pine stands, as well as plantations that have been thinned, are attractive stands for recreational use.

Figure 4-9

Root system of a jack pine in a deep sandy soil. Black and white divisions = 10 cm

K. A. Armson

The eastern white pine is the tree that historically and culturally has been the object of most attention in Ontario. Although characteristic of the Great Lakes – St. Lawrence region, it occurs in all areas of the province except the Boreal barrens. It is very graceful in appearance and grows on a wide variety of soils, in conditions similar to red pine, with which it most frequently occurs. The eastern white pine root system is also similar to that of the red pine in that it can exploit shallow soils and fractured bedrock; it is often associated with red oak whose root system also has this capacity. The logging of eastern white pine, which began commercially in the Ottawa valley in the early to mid 1800s, marked the beginning of Ontario's forest industry.

Eastern White Pine

Other Conifers

Balsam fir is found throughout Ontario except in the very southwest of the province. Tolerant of shade, yet able to grow well in the open, it is a common understory component in both the Great Lakes–St. Lawrence and Boreal regions. Forest fires, depending on their nature and frequency, are a main factor in limiting the occurrence of this species in any forest. Balsam fir is the favoured host of the spruce budworm which is responsible for periodic infestations. Despite these two destructive agents, the balsam fir species regenerates readily.

Eastern hemlock, like balsam fir, is very tolerant of shade, yet will grow well in the open. Characteristic of the Great Lakes–St. Lawrence region, it often occurs in pure stands on moist soils and in northern and eastern aspects. It does not regenerate well on its

Balsam Fir

Figure 4-10
Recreation area in a managed red pine plantation

own, requiring a disturbance such as fire or wind (blowdown) to expose a mineral soil seedbed. This species will also regenerate on rotting logs and stumps. Stands of eastern hemlock are favoured by white-tailed deer as cover in winter since the trees provide browse and minimize snow depth; stands that are frequented in winter on a regular basis are called *deer yards*.

Tamarack (larch) occurs throughout Ontario on a wide range of conditions, but is usually associated with poorly drained organic soils such as peats. It exhibits rapid growth on well-drained soils where it can become established after a disturbance such as a fire. Tamarack is the only native deciduous conifer in Ontario, and its relatively open crowns, even in summer, cast only light shade. In the autumn, the needles turn a brilliant yellow before they fall. Tamarack has a shallow rooting system (similar to black spruce), although it does go somewhat deeper, up to 30 to 60 cm, and its lateral system is very wide spreading.

Eastern white-cedar has a wide range similar to that of tamarack. It also grows on moist and wet soils, although is seldom found on deep organic soils. Typically this species is associated with drainage zones bordering streams and where the soil water is not stagnant. It grows best on neutral to calcareous soils and will invade upland, abandoned areas such as old fields. It is a favoured browse by white-tailed deer and, like eastern hemlock, stands of eastern white-cedar can function as winter deer yards.

Eastern redcedar, in contrast with eastern white-cedar, has a limited range, being common only in southeastern and southwestern Ontario, and small fringe areas bordering southern Georgian Bay. This species can occur on a wide range of soils but typically is found on dry shallow locations and is a colonizer of old fields.

White-cedar

Figure 4-11
Eastern white pine in Algonquin Provincial Park

Photo courtesy of Algonquin Park Museum

K. A. Armson

Inventoried Forest Lands—Age Classes

Areas of Broadleaved (Hardwood) Forest by Age Classes
Areas in thousands ('ooo's) of hectares

Age Class 20 yr. classes	Ontario Crown			Federal	Private	Total
	Parks & Reserves	Other	Total			
0–20	56.1	589.3	645.4	12.8	1103.9	1762.1
21–40	93.8	523.1	616.9	21.1	359.4	997.4
41–60	307.4	1524.9	1832.3	55.3	907.0	2794.6
61–80	399.6	2345.4	2745.0	91.0	1052.5	3888.5
81–100	287.4	1584.4	1871.8	58.2	543.7	2473.7
101–120	123.3	740.5	863.8	20.9	134.9	1019.6
121–140	48.0	264.9	312.9	3.7	17.3	333.9
141–160	50.8	163.8	214.6	1.5	5.9	222.0
161–180	38.4	41.2	79.6	0.1	0.5	80.2
180+	20.5	12.7	33.2	0	0	33.2

Gross Total Volumes—millions of cubic metres

Broadleaved	202.9	1389.2	1592.1	31.2	479.1	2102.4

Mean Annual Increment—thousands of cubic metres per year

Broadleaved	2583.1	18610.2	21193.3	440.0	7142.9	28776.2

Broadleaved (Hardwood) Age Classes by Ownership

Areas in thousands of hectares

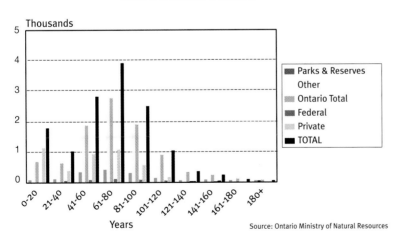

Source: Ontario Ministry of Natural Resources

Figure 4-12
A hemlock stand
N.B. white pine stump

Broadleaved Trees

Trembling Aspen

With the exception of black willow, a tree found from southern Georgian Bay throughout southwestern Ontario and in southeastern Ontario, other native willows—Bebb willow, shining willow and pussy willow—are shrubs or shrubby trees which occur over most of the province. Bebb willow is often called "diamond" willow; in northern Ontario it is made into ornaments by Native Peoples.

Ontario has four native poplars, including two aspens. Trembling aspen is found throughout the province in all three forest regions, while largetooth aspen is limited to the Great Lakes–St. Lawrence and Deciduous regions. Both may be found in pure stands or mixed with other conifer or deciduous species. Aspens commonly occur as clones, reproducing vegetatively, especially after a disturbance which leaves their shallow root systems largely intact. Both of Ontario's aspens occur primarily on well-drained to moist soils, seldom in poorly-drained sites. Each species exhibits strong clonal variation in growth and form. Balsam poplar is found throughout Ontario. Typically it grows along rivers and streams and, together with trembling aspen was one of the early colonizers following deglaciation. In the spring, its resinous buds emit a pleasant fragrant smell as they open. Eastern cottonwood is essentially confined to the Deciduous region and, like balsam poplar, grows best in moist deep soils such as those found along river and stream sides.

K. A. Armson

Although four species of birch occur naturally in the province, only two—white and yellow birch—are common. Gray birch, although common in the Maritimes, is found only in the extreme southeast portion of Ontario. Cherry birch is known at only one location—on the south shore of Lake Ontario. White birch occurs throughout the province and is also planted as an ornamental. This species is very intolerant of shade, and is usually one of the first trees to occupy newly disturbed areas from fire or cutting. White birch will grow on a wide range of soils and can maintain itself on areas of loose boulders and rocks, such as talus slopes. The rooting system is not deep-going and when trees growing in a closed stand are exposed by removal of surrounding stems of neighbouring trees (birch or other species), the residual trees almost invariably die. White birch sap has about one half to one third the sugar content of sugar maple sap, and can be used to make syrup or other concoctions. The bark of the white birch can be readily peeled in the spring and was used first by Aboriginal peoples to make canoes and utensils.

Figure 4-13
Clones of trembling aspen in forest.
N.B. difference in 'leafing out'.

Yellow birch is a characteristic species of the Great Lakes – St. Lawrence region. It also occurs in the Deciduous region and infrequently in certain sites along the southern portion of the Boreal region. Commonly, this species does not occur in pure stands but as a component with eastern hemlock, eastern white pine and other broadleaved trees. Yellow birch grows well on a range of soils, but does best on well to moderately well-drained medium textured soils with northerly and easterly aspects. This tree has moderately deep-going roots and extensive lateral roots; it regenerates best on mineral soil or decaying logs and stumps. Heavy sugar maple litter will preclude the germination and establishment of this species. Yellow birch is a browse species favoured by white-tailed deer and snowshoe hares.

The maple leaf is Canada's emblem and of the ten species of maple native to Canada, seven occur in Ontario. Five are large trees—sugar, black, red, silver, and Manitoba maples—while mountain maple and striped maple are bushy shrubs or small trees.

Sugar maple is characteristic of the Great Lakes – St. Lawrence region and widespread in the Deciduous region. The gold, orange and red colours of its leaves in the crisp autumn air and sunlight are striking. Sugar maple is one of the few forest trees which can

White Birch

Sugar Maple

reproduce prolifically in its own shade, although the young seedlings still require some form of opening if they are to develop into saplings. The root system is compact with some lateral development. Sugar maple is rarely found on poorly drained or shallow soils; it grows best on deeper well-drained loamy textured materials. The best known product of sugar maple trees is maple syrup; sugar maple sap generally has a sugar content of more than two per cent, although this will vary depending on the season and location. Although sugar maple exhibits genetic variation, because it reproduces so well naturally in forests, the only selection for such differences is for ornamental uses or to improve sugar content.

Black maple, although to all intents and purposes the same as sugar maple, differs in two respects. First, it is virtually restricted to the Deciduous region. Second, it is typically found on moist sites along stream and river banks. Black and sugar maple are known to interbreed.

Red maple has the greatest latitudinal range of any of Ontario's forest trees, ranging from southern Florida to the Boreal region. It will thrive on a range of soils and conditions wider than that of any other tree species. Although typically associated with poorly drained soils, red maple can also be commonly found in shallow soils over bedrock locations with eastern white pine and red oak. It has a flexible root system which usually extends laterally, and is not deep-going. Young red maple are an important browse for wildlife like the white-tailed deer. Red maple shows much variation throughout its range, as might be expected. It, like the silver maple, flowers before the leaves emerge. The brilliant red colour of this species' flowers makes it attractive in the early spring.

Silver maple is a tree of moist soils and swamps in the Deciduous and Great Lakes – St. Lawrence regions. It is also one of the most commonly planted ornamentals in cities and towns, in part because of its large variety of leaf forms and habit. Silver maple flowers are less colourful than those of red maple. The silver maple root system is shallow, one reason why it thrives well on poorly-drained alluvial soils. Manitoba maple only occurs naturally in the most southwest tip of the Deciduous region, but it has been planted throughout southern and central Ontario and is now a "naturalized" escape especially around cities and towns in ravines and

Figure 4-14

A sugar maple bush at syrup time.

Photo courtesy, Clarence F. Coons

K. A. Armson

other wooded places. It is the only maple with a compound leaf of 3 to 9 leaflets. Manitoba maple is often called boxelder, especially in the United States.

Mountain maple and striped maple are usually large shrubs, although they can grow into small trees. This is especially true of striped maple, named for the white stripes on its greenish bark. While mountain maple occurs through all three forest regions, striped maple is limited to the central part of the Great Lakes–St. Lawrence region. Both are understory species, growing on moist soils in mixed wood forests, and an important browse for wildlife.

Ten of the eleven oaks native to Canada occur in Ontario, with Garry oak of coastal British Columbia the one exception. Oaks are classified into two groups—red oaks or white oaks. There are five species in the red oak group: red, black, pin, northern pin and Shumard, and five species in the white oak group: white, swamp white, bur, chinquapin, and dwarf chinquapin. Only red, white and bur are common in the regions in which they occur. The other oaks—black, pin, northern pin, Shumard, swamp white, chinquapin, and dwarf chinquapin are uncommon, found only in very limited locations primarily in the Deciduous region.

Red oak is common in the Deciduous and Great Lakes – St. Lawrence regions, usually in mixed woods with eastern white pine or other broadleaved species. It is intermediate in shade tolerance and has a strong root system capable of exploiting both deep soils and shallow soils over fractured bedrock. Established seedlings, although damaged by browsing or fire, retain their ability to resprout from dormant buds. The cycle of damage and resprouting may occur over a period of years, so that when favourable conditions for top growth occur, as an opening in the forest canopy, the plant has a large root system already well-established and rapid growth may ensue.

Black oak is generally similar to red oak but is most common to areas in the southwest of the Deciduous region.

Pin oak grows mainly on poorly drained soils and, with northern pin oak and Shumard oak, occurs only in limited areas in the Niagara Peninsula and to the north of Lake Erie.

White oak is primarily a tree of the Deciduous region but it can also occur in the south central and southeastern portions of the Great Lakes – St. Lawrence region south of the Canadian Shield (Figure 3-1). White oak grows best on deep well-drained soils, usually in mixed wood stands. Bur oak is the most common of the

White Oak

White Elm

white oak group occurring throughout the Deciduous and Great Lakes – St. Lawrence regions. It has a deep-going, coarse root system capable of exploiting a wide range of both deep and shallow soils. It will grow on soils that seasonally range from very wet to very dry conditions and is relatively resistant to ground fires because of its thick bark. Swamp white oak, as its name implies, grows on imperfectly to poorly-drained soils, while chinquapin and dwarf chinquapin oaks occur only in dry locations. All three are small to medium sized trees of very limited occurrence in the extreme south of the Deciduous region. The acorns of all the oaks are a choice food for many small and large animals.

American beech is, like sugar maple, characteristic of the Great Lakes – St. Lawrence region but occurs throughout the Deciduous region. It is one of the most tolerant of shade trees, and has a root system similar to, but shallower than that of sugar maple with which it is commonly found. American beech is uncommon on poorly drained soils occurring mainly on well-drained, moderately deep to deep soils. It is the only large broadleaved tree which retains a smooth bark, and that is grey coloured. On large trees, crops of beech nuts may be produced every 2 to 8 years. When such "mast" crops occur, they provide food for a wide range of animals, including bears which will climb to get at the nut-carrying branches, leaving evidence of their intrusion on the smooth trunk (Figure 4-15).

Elm was one of the earliest colonizing species on deglaciated lands in Ontario. White elm, which is the most widespread of the three elm species native to this province, is found in all three forest regions, although not in the far northwest part of the Boreal region. White elm grows to a large size especially on moist deep soils, although it can be found on a wide range of soil textures, depths and drainage conditions. It was one of rural Ontario's most common hedgerow trees until the 1960s and 1970s when it was exposed to the introduced Dutch elm disease (*Ceratocystis ulmi*), a fungus which plugs the xylem vessels thus preventing water movement to the upper tree parts. Moderately shade tolerant, white elm grows best in the open, and has a flexible root system that varies with the soils in which it grows. Its characteristic umbrella form made the elm a desirable tree for parks and urban planting.

Rock elm is uncommon but can be found in the Deciduous region and small areas in the southcentral and southeastern parts of the Great Lakes – St. Lawrence region. Typically, it is found on

Figure 4-15
Trunk of American beech showing bear claw marks

K. A. Armson

well-drained loamy soils or finer textured soils over limestone. It is readily recognized by the conspicuous corky ridges that develop on its branches. Slippery elm, a tree of the Deciduous region and the extreme southeast of the Great Lakes – St. Lawrence region is the third elm species in the province. It is not common and occurs mainly along stream and riverbanks on moist alluvial soils.

Another tree related to the elms, with the same distribution as slippery elm, but less common is hackberry, which has been used as a substitute for elm in landscaping.

Ironwood, often called "hornbeam" is a small tree of the Deciduous and Great Lakes – St. Lawrence regions. It is a common constituent in mixed wood forests, and its hard tough wood was often used by loggers for axe handles when hickory was not available.

Basswood is a large tree which grows in mixed-wood stands throughout the Deciduous and Great Lakes – St. Lawrence regions. Typically it is found on deep moist soils on north and easterly aspects, and has an extensive root system. Basswood will sprout readily from stumps, after cutting or fire, and produces several large stems from one root system. The wood is white, relatively soft and uniform in texture and is used for wood carving. Its yellowish-white flowers are fragrant and attractive to bees and other insects.

Basswood

Black ash is another broadleaved tree that moved rapidly into Ontario following the retreat of the continental ice sheet. It is wide-spread through all regions on wet soils. It may occur in pure stands but, more usually, is associated with other swamp species such as black spruce, eastern white-cedar or swamp broadleaved trees like silver maple.

White ash occurs on upland soils in the Deciduous and Great Lakes – St. Lawrence regions and has a root system that can exploit deep soils. It is relatively intolerant of shade and regenerates only under openings in a forest canopy. Red ash has a similar range to white ash but is usually found on deep moist soils, and, like black ash, can withstand periodic flooding. Blue ash, the fourth ash species native to Ontario, is recognized by its four-sided twigs. It is relatively rare, being limited to a few isolated locations in the southern part of the Deciduous region and is designated as a threatened species in Canada.

Ontario has two groups of nut trees; both are limited in their distribution, primarily to the Deciduous region and, within it, to isolated occurrences. All are intolerant of shade. Black walnut and

Black Ash

Alien Invaders

Introduced pests and diseases often cause widespread damage to native species that have little or no resistance to them. Dutch elm disease came into North America in New York on logs from Europe. It is a fungus disease that relies on bark beetles to carry its spores from one tree to another. Two beetles are involved, one that is native and the other introduced from Europe in 1904 and now widespread. Thus conditions that are favourable for the beetles to lay their eggs in elms enhance the spread of the disease. Injured or unhealthy branches and trees are favoured by female beetles in laying their eggs under the bark. The first sign of the disease is a yellowing, then wilting of leaves and dying of the affected branches and subsequently the entire tree. Elms show a variable degree of resistance to the disease. Some can sustain repeated infections; others seem immune and a larger proportion have succumbed. However, unlike the depredation of the chestnut blight, elms are still a part of Ontario's forests and landscapes, albeit less than before the 1960s.

butternut can be found in the first group. The second group contains four hickory trees. Butternut and bitternut hickory are sporadic in the Deciduous and the southern and southeastern parts of the Great Lakes – St. Lawrence region off the Canadian Shield. Black walnut is very uncommon in southern woods, although there have been successful plantations of it in recent years, often mixed with eastern white pine. Bitternut and shagbark hickories have similar distribution to butternut. Red and shellbark hickories are limited to a few scattered locations north of Lake Erie. All these trees tend to have tap roots and favour deep well-drained soils for best growth. Their nuts are favoured food by wildlife, and black walnuts by humans.

Five cherry trees are indigenous to Ontario. Two, pin and choke, are small trees or shrubs, and occur throughout all three forest regions. They flower profusely in early spring and their red fruits are favoured by birds and other animals. Both flourish following physical disturbance of the soil where their seeds may lie buried for years. Two plums, the Canada plum and American plum, are small trees. Canada plum is widely distributed in the Deciduous and southern part of the Great Lakes – St. Lawrence regions whereas American plum is in the Deciduous region only. The only large forest cherry tree is the black cherry, occurring in the Deciduous region and the southern portion of the Great Lakes – St. Lawrence region. Black cherry will grow on a wide range of soils excluding very dry and wet situations. It is intolerant of shade and has an extensive, somewhat shallow root system extending usually not more than 60 cm in depth. Serviceberries are small trees or shrubs which occur in all three regions and are notable for their white flowers which are showy and appear in the spring before the leaves of other trees have emerged.

Several trees limited to Ontario's Deciduous region are uncommon to rare. These species are characteristic of the forests in the southeastern United States and are often referred to as "Carolinian" trees. Tulip tree is the most common and occurs in deciduous woodlands, regenerating well after disturbances such as cutting. It is an extremely rapid grower and produces straight branch-free boles. Sassafras is a smaller tree with twigs that emit a strong odour. Sycamore grows to a large size and is found on more poorly-drained soils along streams; it can be long-lived, up to 200 years or more. A smaller tree of seasonally poorly-drained low lying areas in woodlands is the black gum. It is intolerant of shade

K. A. Armson

and, like poplar, will regenerate from root suckers after cutting. Paw paw, cucumber-tree and the Kentucky-coffee tree are very uncommon and are only found in the extreme south of the Deciduous region. Red bud is another small tree that is rare naturally, but has been planted for its early spring red flowers.

The relative proportion of occurrence for some of the main tree species found in Ontario is shown in Figures 4-16 a and b. A large number of species occur throughout much of Ontario's forests as shrubs, and sometimes as small trees. Several species of alders, mainly but not exclusively associated with streams and wetlands, are ubiquitous. The showy mountain-ash, and American mountain-ash have white flowers and red fruits which provide splashes of colour, especially in the Boreal forest. Several species of hawthorns predominantly in the Deciduous and Great Lakes – St. Lawrence regions (but limited to the central and southern portions of the Boreal forest), are often found in openings and most commonly on old farm lands. In the fall, the bright red and orange colours of staghorn sumac leaves are common in the Deciduous and Great Lakes – St. Lawrence regions where this species grows in clusters in openings and along roadsides. Blueberries are one of the most common types of low bushes in the province, particularly throughout the Boreal and Great Lakes – St. Lawrence regions. They are intolerant of shade and grow profusely after major disturbances such as fire—especially on coarser-textured well-drained soils. Wild blueberries are an important commercial crop in northern Ontario and, of course, provide food for wildlife in the late summer—especially black bears.

Many species of mosses, lichens, herbaceous and other plants carpet the floor of Ontario's forests, and together with a myriad of other creatures, make them some of the most interesting and dynamic forests in Canada.

Balsam Poplar

Black Walnut

Eastern white pine

Red pine

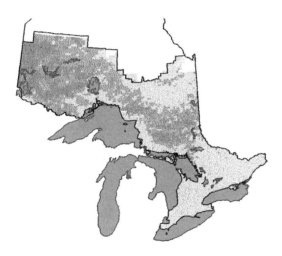

Jack pine

Black spruce

Figure 4-16a Conifer species

Relative occurrence of main conifer species

Charts courtesy of the Ontario Ministry of Natural Resources

K. A. Armson

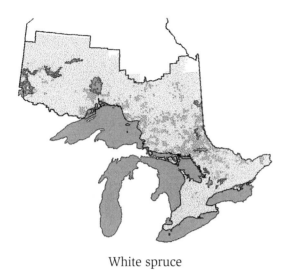

White spruce

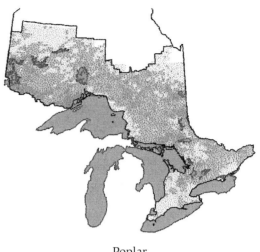

Poplar

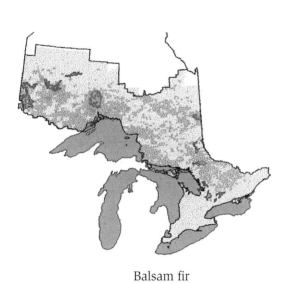

Balsam fir

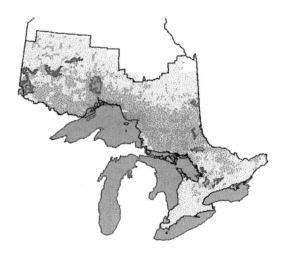

White birch

Figure 4-16a Conifer species

Figure 4-16b Broadleaved species

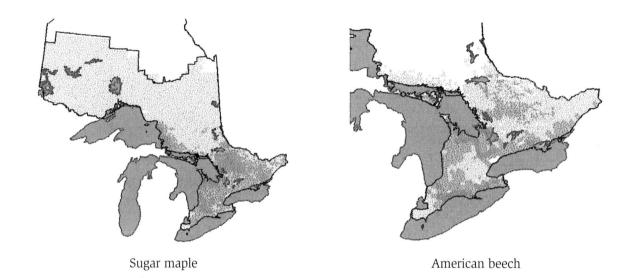

Sugar maple   American beech

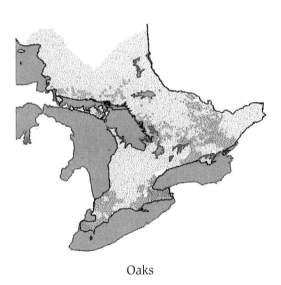

Oaks

Figure 4-16b Broadleaved species

Relative occurrence of main broadleaved species

Charts courtesy of the Ontario Ministry of Natural Resources

K. A. Armson

V

The Life and Times of Ontario's Forests

The Life and Times of Ontario's Forests

The forests of Ontario are continuously subjected to a wide range of factors which affect their nature and growth, development and demise. Many of these factors are non-human and uncontrollable, although their impact on forests and lands may be ameliorated or intensified by human actions. For example, forest fires caused by lightning cannot be prevented, but rapid detection and suppression measures can drastically limit the area and intensities of fires. Although the non-human factors of fire, wind, insects and disease are ever-present and on-going, it is more often the impact of human action which generates the widest response. The removal of trees in urban areas, logging of old-growth forests, and the conversion of woodlands to other uses are frequent rallying points for public concern. What is often not realized is that disturbances, whether non-human or human, have been the norm in forest development for thousands of years; it is the interactions of these disturbances, and their intensities which deserve our attention and study if we are to better understand Ontario's forests and their environment. Although this section separates the non-human and human disturbance factors for simplicity of discussion, it is the interaction of these factors which are most critical and will be stressed.

Non-human

Soils _____

When the continental glacier retreated, it exposed the land's surface. Subsequent changes throughout the millennia introduced many sets of factors to influence the nature, growth, development and death of Ontario's forests, and the plants and animals they comprise. One fact is clear, nothing remains static—even though to an observer it may seem so. Climate is a predominant influence. Temperature and moisture regimes control to a large extent, the physiological activities of plants and animals, as well as the rates and nature of physical and chemical reactions in the forest environment. Interactions between climatic factors, forest organisms and the physiographic features of the landscape in which they occur over time, result in specific forests as well as determining the soils in which they grow. Soils are often regarded as stable surface materials on which plants grow, but they should be seen as the result of the interaction between climate, geological materials, and organisms—plants and animals—and the processes—chemical, physical and biological—that occur over time. These interactions and processes are constantly changing; so does the soil.

When the ice front retreated, exposed geological materials were subjected to periodic, seasonal freezing and thawing. As a result, vertical wedges of looser material made it easier for the deep-going roots of the earliest plants to establish themselves in this, the periglacial zone. Successions of plants added organic matter to the soil, both as litter at the surface—the *forest floor*—and below the surface—as dead roots. These organic additions provided a food source for a multitude of lesser plants and animals, which in turn contributed further to the soil's organic component.

K. A. Armson

The presence of water and its movement in the soil (depending on temperature regimes), ensures the chemical and physical weathering of soil minerals and the movement of products from these processes.

Essentially, the process of soil development consists of:

a) *Additions*—such as organic matter and precipitation;

b) *Losses*—when water containing products of weathering—organic and inorganic—leaves the soil as runoff, or passes through the body of soil to lower zones;

c) *Translocation*—when materials in solution or solids are moved within the soil body;

d) *Transformations*—when organic and inorganic materials are changed in either their physical or chemical state, or both.

Soil is dependent on plants for its formation. It also creates conditions which affect the rooting environment for vegetation. Although the surficial geological materials in which Ontario's forest soils have developed are often quite thick, extending to several metres, the soil bodies themselves are quite thin, usually less than one metre in depth. A vertical cross-section exposes the soil's profile and its sequence of layers, or horizons, which are differentiated by colour and other properties.

Ontario has six main classes of forest soils (technically, these are termed Orders in the Canadian System of Soil Classification) as illustrated in Figures 5-1 to 5-6.

Four soils (Figures 5-1 – 5-4) represent the most common, well-drained to imperfectly drained forest soils. The Brunisols (Figure 5-1) have a forest floor with some litter (L) and partially decomposed material (F) but there is sufficient soil organism activity to create a thin layer (Ah) of mixed minerals and humus. The weathering of the soil minerals results in some movement of iron and other materials so that there may be a very thin silica-rich whitish zone often discontinuous below the Ah. The main body of the soil is reddish brown due to the weathering of minerals and accumulation of those products *in situ*. Brunisols are associated mainly with forests in the Great Lakes – St. Lawrence region, in areas at the southern and eastern margins of the Canadian Shield, but they can also be found in the Boreal forest, particularly under deciduous forest cover. Typically, Brunisols are moderately acidic (pH 5.5); depending on the nature of the geological materials, the texture and stone content will vary.

Figure 5-1 A Brunisol

Figure 5-2 A Podzol

Figure 5-3 A Luvisol

Figure 5-4 A Regosol (lithosol)

K. A. Armson

Figure 5-5 Podzol soil showing disturbance from windthrown trees

Figure 5-6 A Gleysol

Figure 5-7 An Organic soil (peat)

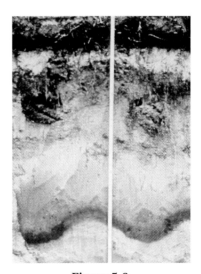

Figure 5-8
A bisequum of one profile (podzol) developed in the top of another (grey-brown podzolic),

Photo courtesy Agriculture Canada

Red Oak

(Quercus rubra)

Located in Harwich Township, Kent County, this tree has a diameter of 194 centimetres with a height of 31.1 metres.

Podzols (Figure 5-2) are major types of soil within the Boreal and Great Lakes – St. Lawrence forest regions. They are acidic (pH < 5), and characterized by a forest floor of litter (L) and partially decomposed organic remains (F)—*mor* humus (Figure 5-10)—sharply delineated from an underlying highly weathered, white, silica-rich mineral horizon (Ae). Below this are horizons of accumulation of weathering products, mainly humic, iron and aluminum, varying in colour from black—to dark brown—dark reddish/yellow brown (Bh–Bf), mainly translocated from the upper Ae horizon. There are many variations within these soils resulting from changes in vegetation over time. Generally, the longer the soils have developed under conifers, the stronger the degree of weathering and more highly developed the soil profile, but the nature of the lesser vegetation also has an effect. For example, ericaceous species result in stronger weathering than most herbaceous vegetation.

The nature and frequency of forest fires result in vegetation changes. Fires reduce the forest floor by burning, leaving minerals such as calcium, magnesium, potassium and phosphorus in the residual ash. These minerals have a profound influence in moderating the intense weathering associated with Podzol development. In addition, dead standing trees—*chicots*—are usually blown down after forest fires. Their roots create a mixing of soil materials (Figure 5-5). This action, over hundreds of centuries, results in a crude form of cultivation, which exposes fresh minerals to weathering and a physical mixing of organic matter and minerals. The result is fresh seedbeds and improved soils for the reestablishment of vegetation. Podzols occur on a wide range of soil textures, from the very coarse sands and gravels to silts and clays.

Luvisols (Figure 5-3) are the major forest soil in the Great Lakes – St. Lawrence forest region south of the Canadian Shield, and in the Deciduous forest region on finer textured soils containing clay. They also occur in the Boreal region in northwest and northeast Ontario on clay materials. These are slightly acid to neutral soils, often with a lower zone of free carbonates. In the southern part of the province, the decomposition of forest litter is rapid, with the previous year's deposition being completely decomposed by late summer. The soils therefore have a transient litter and decomposing forest floor and a well-developed Ah (*mull*) humus type (Figure 5-10). The upper mineral zone is greyish, from which clay has been removed in suspension and redeposited in a

K. A. Armson

layer beneath (Bt). Calcium carbonate from these upper layers is often deposited beneath the Bt as a distinct accumulation.

Regosols (Figure 5-4) are soils in which little weathering and horizon development has occurred. This may happen in freshly exposed or deposited geological materials, or in very shallow materials over bedrock (lithosols). Typically these soils have a forest floor with litter (L), partial decomposition (F), some humus (H), and a limited Ah horizon of mixed humus and mineral materials. In Ontario, Regosols are sporadic in their occurrence and tend to be primarily associated with exposed bedrock, which, if fractured, can support productive forests.

The two remaining types of soils are poorly or very poorly drained. These are the Gleysols and Organic soils. Gleysols (Figure 5-6) are mineral soils that, for periodic or prolonged times, are so saturated with water that chemical reduction of iron and other minerals occurs. Saturation is often a result of a fluctuating water table or from location in a depression. The forest floor has a litter (L) layer and partially decomposed (F) material and there may be some mixing of upper mineral and humus (Ah), but these soils are characterized by yellow/reddish brown to blue-grey mottling within 50 cm of the surface. They occur predominantly in areas of low relief. Organic soils (Figure 5-7) are comprised mainly of partially decomposed to well-decomposed organic remains, and are saturated with water most of the time. They vary greatly according to the physical structure of their organic material, which is largely dependent on the nature and degree of decomposition. These soils constitute what are described as peat, bog or muck soils, and although, generally, they form in depressions and areas of low relief, they can also form when there is impeded drainage in well-drained soil areas. Organic soils are common in the Boreal forest, mostly supporting black spruce and tamarack tree species. Where organic soils develop on gentle slopes with lateral movement of the water, they are very productive; alders are usually a shrub component of such sites.

The distribution of the six main types of soil found in Ontario is shown in Figure 5-9. Within each of the major areas identified, there are many variations in soil profiles dependent on local differences in topography and drainage, and the effects of plants and animals. Many differences are time dependent and, as one soil profile develops, it may establish conditions for a second set of soil forming processes such that one distinct type of soil develops

Grafted Sugar Maple

A short distance south of Hall Road East, Binbrook, adjacent to Chippawa Creek, is a unique sugar maple. Two trees have grafted at a height of 3.6 metres and continue as a single trunk to a height of 24 metres. According to one historian, a registered Tuscarora, these trees were probably grafted together as a territorial marker for the Cayuga First Nation. This tree was designated as a Heritage Tree under the Ontario Heritage Act in 1982.

within another earlier one. These soils are referred to as bisequums. An example is given in Figure 5-8. The importance of the forest vegetation in soil development cannot be overemphasized. Although the geological surficial materials set the physical dimensions and determine many of the physical and chemical properties, the development and dynamics of the organic contributions are often key in determining fertility and particularly the nature of the forest floor. These are especially important where major non-human and human disturbances occur. The three main kinds of humus types—mull, moder and mor Figure (5-10)—illustrate the most significant features of forest floors.

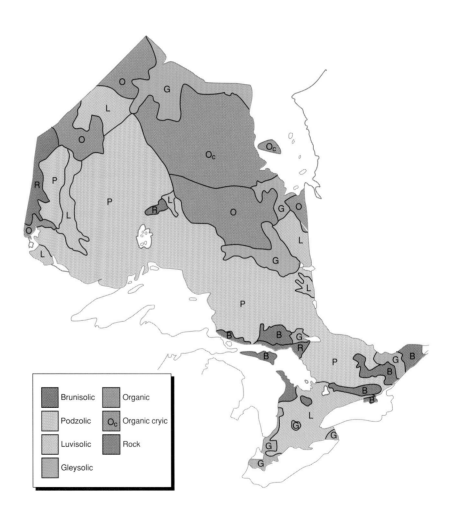

Legend:
- Brunisolic
- Podzolic
- Luvisolic
- Gleysolic
- Organic
- Oc Organic cryic
- Rock

Figure 5-9 Distribution of the main classes (Orders) of forest soils in Ontario.

Based on information from Soils in Canada, 1977.

K. A. Armson

The forest floor of a mull humus usually has a continuous litter layer for the fall, winter and into mid summer; by this time much of the material has been decomposed. This is the way in which nutrients are recycled from vegetation back into the soil, maintaining its fertility. If the soil surface is exposed to erosive forces from disturbances when the surface litter has been largely decomposed, as in mid to late summer, serious losses in fertility can result. This is why major removal of tree cover, especially crown canopies, on such soils can degrade the soil's productivity. In contrast, the mor humus, characterized by an accumulation of litter and partially decomposed surface material "locks up" many nutrients in relatively unavailable form. It is the non-human disturbances such as fire which may consume as much as one half of the forest floor, releasing mineral ash, part of which may blow away but part of which serves as an inorganic fertilizer. Human disturbances, such as silvicultural clearfelling, have a modified but somewhat similar effect by exposing the soil to increased moisture and temperature, hence increasing the rates of decomposition. As long as a portion of the forest floor remains, the soil is largely protected from the normal erosive forces of wind and water. Moder humus, as its name implies, is a form between mull and mor, but its rates of decomposition are more rapid than in mor humus and, consequently, so is the nutrient cycling.

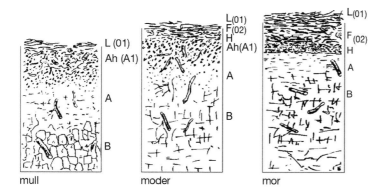

Figure 5-10 Mull, Moder and Mor humus types (Source: Armson, K.A. Forest Soils, 1977)

Figure 5-11
Aerial view of a large (130,000 ha) forest blowdown in northwestern Ontario

K. A. Armson

Wind and Ice _____

Wind can be both ameliorating and destructive to forests. In exposed low-lying depressions where cold air can accumulate and frost occurs, a wind can minimize, if not prevent, damage to susceptible vegetation. More commonly, however, it is the destructive force which is usually associated with windthrow of individual trees, or less frequently with the blowdown of entire forest stands. Large, biologically over-mature individual trees with weakened root systems are most susceptible to windthrow. This is a common form of disturbance in the broadleaved forests of the Deciduous region and in portions of the Great Lakes – St. Lawrence region. Such windthrows result in an accumulation of tree stems and partial roots on the forest floor, in addition to the turning up and mixing of soil brought to the surface by the roots. Windthrow of this type is essentially a chronic form of disturbance providing small openings for regeneration or allowing younger trees to grow more rapidly. Tornadoes, on the other hand, are erratic, relatively infrequent, affect very limited areas in the forest, and often result more in stem breakage, especially in younger stands. In the northern Boreal forest, windstorms which blow down large forest areas (Figure 5-11), result in large amounts of trees on the forest floor, creating conditions ripe for major fires because of fuel loading. Large blowdowns also become major sites for build-ups of insect populations, such as bark beetles, which can then spread into surrounding forest stands.

The destructive effects of wind are intensified when combined with ice storms. Light ice storms occur relatively frequently in much of Ontario, particularly during early winter, and result in a pruning of dead and dying branches. Very infrequently, as happened in eastern Ontario in January 1998, a severe ice storm occurs, which destroys many trees, particularly the broadleaved, and causes major losses in woodlots and sugar bushes (Figure 3-12).

Figure 5-12
Aerial view of forest burnt in 1961(right) and 1968(left).
Photo 1968, Blackstone Lake, northwestern Ontario

K. A. Armson

Fire _____

Fire resulting from lightning has been a most important factor in much of Ontario's forests through the millennia. In the Boreal region and large parts of the Great Lakes – St. Lawrence forests, it has been the main factor both in destroying forests while at the same time creating conditions for regeneration and development of new forests. The magnitude of any fire, its intensity, frequency, duration, time of year, the kind of forest being burnt and its nature—whether by a ground or crown fire—all contribute to the effects and, thus, the resultant forest.

Crown fires in mature to over-mature conifer forests of jack pine and black spruce invariably result in new forests of the same species, although the species proportions may change. Ground fires through polewood stands of these or other species, including broadleaved trees, usually result in the killing off of the smaller, thinner barked trees, thinning the forest so that the growth of the larger residual trees is increased. Unless there are seed crops present, fires through white and red pine forests usually result in much higher proportions of deciduous species such as white birch and poplars. Wildfires are often very large in extent and, their effects can vary with the physiography, drainage, and vegetation over which the fire ranges, producing distinctive patterns. In addition to consuming standing timber and other vegetation, fires also burn the upper part of the forest floor—the surface litter and a portion of the partially decomposed organic material under it. Typically, a severe forest fire only reduces the thickness of the forest floor up to about one half in the Boreal and Great Lakes – St. Lawrence regions. Roots of species like poplar, which are mainly in the upper soil, especially in more humus types, can be killed by severe ground fires. Consequently, poplar will be less represented in the new forest.

Prior to human interference, the frequency of major fires was every 50 to 80 years in many forests—less intensive fires, like ground fires occurred more frequently. Annual forest areas burned in Ontario since 1917, when the province began keeping routine records, are shown in Figure 5-13. During this 82 year period, the total cumulative area burned was equivalent to one fifth of the total forest area of the province (Figure 5-14).

Large fires produce considerable ash containing mineral nutrients such as calcium and potassium. While some of this is left on the forest floor producing a period of higher soil fertility for up to ten years, the remainder is carried aloft in the smoke and eventually washes to the surface elsewhere. Some lakes in Ontario's forests periodically have acidity degrees lowered by such ash deposits, thus affecting water quality.

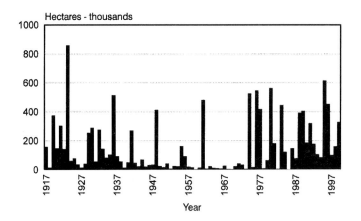

Figure 5-13

Burned forest areas, 1917–1999.

Source: Ontario Ministry of Natural Resources

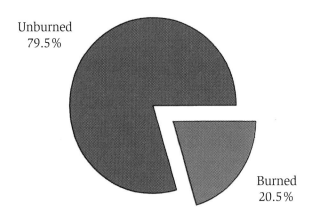

Figure 5-14

Proportion of burned area to total forest area, 1917–1999.

K. A. Armson

Insects and Diseases _____

The spruce budworm (*Choristoneura fumiferana* Clem.) is the most destructive pest of Ontario's spruce and balsam fir forests. It is a native insect which has attacked balsam fir and spruce presumably since these species first appeared in the province. From the early 18th to the late 19th centuries, major spruce budworm outbreaks occurred at an average frequency of 29 years. These outbreaks still occur today, but are left to take a natural course unless they threaten timber stands required for harvest in the short term, recreational parks or small forest areas of high value—like tree seed orchards. Control is done with aerial application of a bacterium (*Bacillus thuringiensis* -Bt); the object is not to kill all the insects but to maintain the foliage of the trees under attack.

One beneficial effect of defoliation is that other less-susceptible species underneath the balsam fir canopy can be released, to grow more rapidly as light is let in by foliage removal, or even the death of the attacked trees.

A similar insect, the jack pine budworm (*Choristoneura pinus pinus* Free.), probably caused considerable damage in the past, but owing to lack of records and the fact that jack pine was not in major demand by the forest industry until after World War II (1939–1945), less is known of the history of this pest's damage. Recent outbreaks have been treated as for spruce budworm. Both spruce and jack pine budworm cause loss of foliage, hence reduction in growth and tree mortality. When large areas are affected, the standing dead trees provide an important fuel source for forest fires. Historically, forests subjected to major attacks by budworms have subsequently been devastated by burning. Immediately following the killing of trees by either insects or fire, other insects, primarily bark beetles, rapidly invade the site, before moving on to live trees in the surrounding area.

The main insect pest of eastern white pine is the white pine weevil (*Pissodes strobi* Peck). Although it is indigenous, the weevil did not become a serious problem until the early 1900s when eastern white pine plantings began to be used in reforestation of open lands. The weevil causes the death of the tree's terminal shoots. When this is done year after year, the pine becomes bushy but is seldom killed. Usually, white pines outgrow the effects of the weevil but the result is poor form and knotty timber. The female weevil is attracted to shoots with thick stems (which are charac-

Insects are not all bad Defoliation by certain insects can have beneficial effects in forests. Their frass or droppings add nutrients to the soil. The openings in the tree crowns resulting from the loss of foliage allows more light and increased rainfall and temperature to reach the ground. Both tree regeneration and herbaceous plants benefit and will increase in growth. A net result is that for a period of a year or more the rate of decomposition in the forest floor increases, with positive effects on soil fertility.

Figure 5-15
Balsam fir killed by
spruce budworm

teristic for trees growing in the open) to lay her eggs. White pines under partial shade grow less rapidly, have thinner shoots, and are less subject to weevil attack. Areas with little to no natural white pine, and no weevils, present little risk of attack for eastern white pine reforestation projects planted in the open.

The pine shoot borer (*Eucosma gloriola* Heinr.) is an insect which attacks terminals of pines, especially jack pine. The borer also kills the terminal shoot but is less persistent than the white pine weevil. Trees can become deformed over a shorter period—two to three years.

A multitude of insects feed on conifers—sawflies, which eat the foliage of spruce and pines, bark beetles, cone insects, and root-feeding pests. The buildup of these pest populations and consequent degree of damage, are dependent on many factors in addition to the presence of suitable host trees. Weather, particularly certain sequences of precipitation and temperature, the host tree's stage of development, as well as that of the surrounding trees, and predators can all be contributing factors.

The most common defoliator of broadleaved trees in Ontario is the forest tent caterpillar *(Malacosoma disstria* Hbn.) which despite its name, does not form a tent. It is a native pest that prefers poplar leaves but will attack most other broadleaved trees during major outbreaks, which occur at intervals of 10 to 12 years. When populations have been at their peak, masses of caterpillars crossing roads and railway tracks have been known to slow down if not halt traffic. Poplars, especially aspens are weakened when defoliated, but most will not succumb. With defoliation of the upper canopy, conifer regeneration in the understory will respond in growth to the increased light, precipitation and temperature afforded.

The eastern tent caterpillar (*Malacosoma americana* Fabricius) does form a tent and exists at chronic levels, for the most part attacking pin and choke cherries—where their tents are conspicuous. Outbreaks do occur, and other broadleaved tree species can be attacked as well, but the eastern tent caterpillar is not generally considered a serious forest pest.

The gypsy moth (*Lymantria dispar* L.) was introduced from Europe into the United States in 1869, and was thought to have been destroyed until the mid 1920s and 1930s outbreaks in Québec and New Brunswick. In the northeastern United States, the gypsy moth has been a major defoliator of many broadleaved tree species,

K. A. Armson

particularly oaks. It will feed on just about any foliage during a major outbreak, including that of agricultural crops. It also feeds on many conifers and is particularly destructive of eastern hemlock. The gypsy moth was first found in Ontario in 1969. There was a major outbreak in central and eastern sections of the province during the mid 1980s.

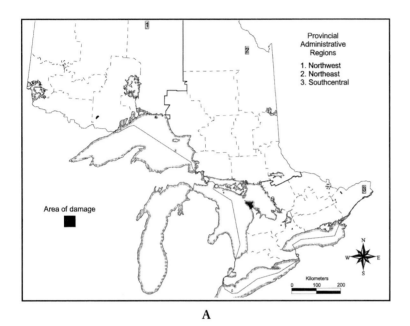

A

B

Figure 5-16
Defoliation by spruce budworm,
a) 1967 – 79,927 ha.;
b) 1970 – 2,804,532 ha.

Source: Gordon Howse, Canadian Forest Service

Figure 5-16

Defoliation by spruce budworm,

c) 1975–13,454,067 ha.;

d) 1980–18,850,000 ha.

Source: Gordon Howse, Canadian Forest Service

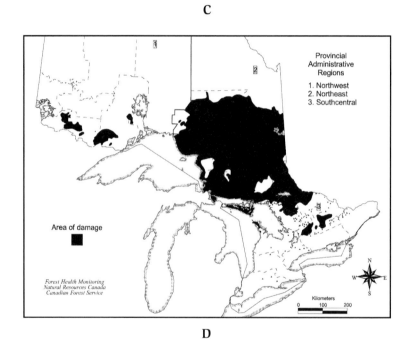

C

D

Although there are a number of insects, such as canker worms, tussock moths, and leaf rollers, that will attack maples, these trees generally are not particularly susceptible to significant insect damage. The most destructive pest is the sugar maple borer (*Glycobius speciosus* Say), a large beetle which lays its eggs in cracks and crevices in the bark; on hatching, the larvae feed on the sapwood over a two-year period.

K. A. Armson

The most ubiquitous tree diseases in the province are those organisms causing root rots which, because of their location, have been called, the *hidden enemy*[1]. It has been estimated that the annual loss to decay in Ontario's forests is 21 million cubic metres of wood, of which 12 million or 57 per cent is attributable to root rots.

The most common root rot, not only in Ontario but in the world, is the shoestring fungus or honey mushroom (*Armillaria obscura*). It exists on woody debris in the soil and can attack virtually all of Ontario's tree species. Typically, it invades live roots of trees by means of rhizomorphs, i.e. fungal strands encased in an outer darkish compacted tissue, hence the name "shoestring." Although it will attack trees of all ages, this rot is particularly evident in young conifer stands, especially where there are relatively fresh hardwood stumps left from cutting or other disturbance.

Another root rot particularly damaging to older white and black spruce trees is the tomentosus root rot (*Inonotus tomentosus*). Tomentosus spreads from an infected tree to its surrounding neighbours. As the roots die off, trees become less windfirm and blow down, creating openings of various sizes in the forest.

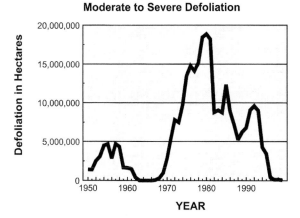

Figure 5-17

Moderate to severe defoliation 1950 to 1999.

Source: Gordon Howse, Canadian Forest Service

Figure 5-18

Windthrown black spruce, weakened by root rot.

Source: R.D. Whitney, Canadian Forest Service

One of the rots particularly damaging to pines is the annosus rot (*Heterobasidion annosum*). It is restricted to southern Ontario and spread in stands by windborne spores which infect freshly cut stumps after thinning has occurred.

The greatest stem damage in conifers is caused by a fungus, *Phellinus pini*. This is a heart rot that causes the wood to be red coloured; hence this fungus is often called red rot. Infection can enter the tree through broken limbs or branch stubs, advancing both up and down the stem. The rate of decay spread is in the order of 5 to 10 cm per year in eastern white pine. Red rot decay can provide sites for cavity nesting birds.

Diseases of the sugar maple seldom kill a tree unless it is young, although infections cause deformities and reduced growth and wood quality. Two of the most common diseases causing cankers on the stems of maples, birches and many other deciduous species are Eutypella canker (*Eutypella parasitica* Davids & Lorenz) and Nectria canker (*Nectria galligena* Bres.). Nectria cankers are readily identified because, as the tree's cells are killed, the canker takes the form of a target and is often referred to as "target canker"(Figure 5-19).

Diseases which depend on an alternation of host plants have an important effect on eastern white pine and jack pine. The blister rust (*Cronartium ribicola* J.C.Fischer) was brought to North America from Europe around about 1900 and spread rapidly throughout the range of eastern white pine. Blister rust spends part of its life cycle on species of gooseberries and currants (*Ribes spp.*) where it does little damage. In mid to late summer pine needles are infected by spores from the Ribes plants. The fungus grows in the conducting tissues of the tree, under its bark, for two years or so. In the spring, the fungus produces large yellow blisters on the cankered area. These are filled with spores which become windborne and infect any Ribes plant in the vicinity. The cycle begins anew. Small trees are usually killed when the canker girdles the stem. On larger trees, often only the infected branches are killed, although the growth of the tree is slowed and ultimately death may occur. Since the disease cannot spread from

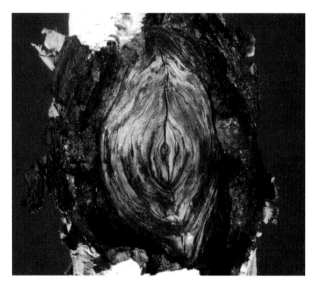

Figure 5-19

"Target" canker caused by Nectria galligena on white birch

Photo courtesy, Great Lakes Forestry Centre, Canadian Forest Service

K. A. Armson

one pine to another, control measures at the stand level consist of physically pulling out Ribes bushes. This practice, is impractical over large forest areas.

The sweetfern blister rust (*Cronartium comptoniae* Arth.), as its name implies, infects sweetferns (*Comptonia peregrina* L. (Coult.)) which grow throughout central and northern Ontario on well-drained soils in forest areas where jack pine also occurs. Another host of this rust is sweet gale (*Myrica gale* L.) which grows adjacent to water and in swamps, and is much less important as a source of the disease for jack pine. Typically, the rust infects young jack pine in the seedling stage or during the first few years of growth. It may form a canker, which appears as a swelling at the base of the stem, and kill the small tree. More often, the rust lives within the pine for many years, not apparent until a canker appears as a longitudinal swelling in the lower part of the bole of the tree. Canker development some 20 or more years after initial infection seems related to stress on the tree due to an imbalance in water supply—as often occurs when jack pines are in a polewood stage of development. While growth loss will occur, the tree usually does not die. The deformity in the lower stem, however, reduces its value for sawlogs.

The pine gall rust (*Endocronartium harknessii*) does not require an alternate host but will spread from jack pine to jack pine. It produces a round gall that can girdle the stem in small trees, killing the pine. In larger trees this rust is more common on branches, although it can occur on the main stem. Pine gall rust is

Figure 5-20
Artist's conk, Ganoderma applanatum.

Photo courtesy, Great Lakes Forestry Centre, Canadian

Forest Service

particularly prevalent in northwestern Ontario jack pines, causing much deformity in crown development.

There are many diseases which infect both conifer and broadleaved species causing discolouration or decay of internal wood. The first sign that a tree is infected is the presence of "conks"—shelf-like fruiting bodies of fungus on the tree's stem. *Oxyporus populinus* occurs on many species but is particularly prevalent on maples where it is responsible for degrading wood quality. The false tinder fungus (*Phellinus igniarius*) attacks many broadleaved species, especially aspen poplars and birches—which are particularly susceptible. The best known disease of this type is *Ganoderma applanatum* (Figure 5-20), commonly called "shelf" or "artist's" conk because it is large and has a smooth surface which can be painted. This disease infects a wide range of broadleaved and conifer species—primarily maples, American beech and oaks in Ontario.

Most of the insect pests and disease organisms that affect Ontario's forest are chronic. It is those insects and diseases, which for one reason or another, periodically increase in significant numbers and impact, that are classed as epidemic and attract the greatest attention and concern. Mostly we take our trees and forests for granted. Insects and microorganisms that occur in Ontario's forests, only a few of which we label as "pests," are responsible for the transformation of organic material—living and dead—above and below ground, and are vital in the continuing cycle of growth and decay. As forest conditions change over time, the prevalence or effects of individual species or groups of organisms will alter. Ultimately, all trees succumb to decay and the longer they live, the more susceptible they are, some species more so than others. Aspen poplar and balsam fir have shorter life spans than sugar maple and eastern white pine, but much depends on the conditions under which they grow. Generally, trees growing on the most productive sites will not only grow faster but mature earlier; consequently the onset of maturity and decay will occur earlier than for the same species on less productive sites.

Photo courtesy Algonquin Provincial Park

K. A. Armson

Human

Pre-European _____

Humans made their first appearance in Ontario some 12,000 years ago as the continental ice sheet retreated. Their arrival was contemporary with that of the first tree species—spruce and willow. For many millennia, the human impact, among others, was minimal to non-existent. It was not until about one to two thousand years ago that changes reflecting human activities occurred in some forested areas. With the arrival of Europeans in the 17th century, the activity pace accelerated and it has continued to the present. Although some of the human activity has resulted in major changes, including total forest removal in parts of the province, particularly southern Ontario, the nature of the forests and their species in the large remaining portions of the province has remained remarkably similar over the centuries. Figure 5-21 shows a generalized time scale for human occupation in southern Ontario over the past 12,000 years.

The Paleo-Indians, were the earliest inhabitants of southern Ontario. They were mobile hunters in what would have been semi-open boreal parkland during the time of mastodons and woolly mammoths, long since extinct, and of caribou. It is thought that the Paleo-Indian population was small, consisting of nuclear families who combined into bands of 45 to 75 people. Evidence of their existence can be found in three locations in southern Ontario, one at Parkhill (inland from Ipperwash Beach on the shore of Lake Huron), the Fisher site (inland from what is now southern Georgian Bay), and Rice Lake, south of Peterborough. Fluted point projectiles and scrapers made from quartzite or chert are the main artifacts associated with these locations. Paleo-Indians probably used primitive means of transport—some form of sled or canoe—over ice, snow and water. As the ice retreated farther north, boreal forests succeeded the more open park land forest, and the Paleo-Indians were succeeded in southern Ontario by Archaic peoples. Not much is known about them but that they were also hunter-gatherers and thus would have had minimal impact on the forests in which they lived.

The early Archaic gave rise to the Laurentian Archaic who occupied southern Ontario in a forest not unlike what we have today. There is evidence that during the middle to latter part of the Archaic period, people constructed fish weirs, and collected nuts—walnuts, butternuts and hickory nuts. They also were involved in the exchange of marine shells from the east, and copper from Lake Superior. To the north, on the Canadian Shield, the peoples were known as Shield Archaic, and existed in essentially boreal forests. Towards the middle and late Archaic period, the climate in Ontario became much warmer, particularly in the central and northern areas, and it is during this period that peoples from the west moved into areas on the north shore of what is now Lake Superior and the north shore of Lake Huron and Manitoulin Island. This warming period (hypsithermal or altithermal) between approximately six and a half and four thousand years BP, as already noted,

Figure 5-21
Generalized time scale of human occupation in southern Ontario

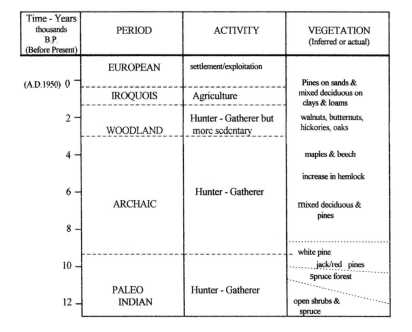

Time - Years thousands B.P. (Before Present)	PERIOD	ACTIVITY	VEGETATION (Inferred or actual)
(A.D. 1950) 0	EUROPEAN	settlement/exploitation	Pines on sands & mixed deciduous on clays & loams
	IROQUOIS	Agriculture	
2	WOODLAND	Hunter - Gatherer but more sedentary	walnuts, butternuts, hickories, oaks
4			maples & beech
			increase in hemlock
6	ARCHAIC	Hunter - Gatherer	mixed deciduous & pines
8			
10			white pine / jack/red pines / Spruce forest
12	PALEO INDIAN	Hunter - Gatherer	open shrubs & spruce

K. A. Armson

resulted in tree species from the Great Lakes–St. Lawrence forests moving farther north, as we discussed earlier in the case of eastern white pine.

The Laurentian Archaic were succeeded by Woodland peoples from approximately three thousand years ago to 500 A.D. It is during this period that populations increased, and there was a more sedentary type of life. The latter part of this period was characterized by the introduction of technologies and ideas from Native Peoples to the south (present day Ohio and Michigan) in Ontario. The earliest examples of known pottery, bows and arrows were found from this period, as well as burial mounds, at Rice Lake and Rainy River. Burial mounds would continue to be used until the early 1600s, but only in northern Ontario. They were no longer being built in southern Ontario by 500 A.D.. From 500 A.D. (approximately 1,500 yrs BP) until contact with Europeans in the mid-1500s A.D., the northern forests were occupied by Algonquian-speaking peoples—Cree, Ojibway and Algonquin—successors to the Woodland people.

In southern Ontario, sometime between 3,000 BP and 1,500 BP (1,000 B.C.–500 A.D.), the practice of agriculture was introduced, first with corn (maize), later with squash, beans, sunflowers and tobacco as the basic crops. The expansion of native agriculture in southern Ontario probably took considerable time, but by about 800 years ago (1200 A.D.) it was generally widespread, and with it was a significant increase in population. It is at this time that the first major human cultural impacts occurred on Ontario's forests, setting in place land use patterns that have had an influence to this day, not only in terms of the forest but more especially in the mythology which has given rise to major errors in our understanding of these forests.

During this period of developing agriculture in the first millennium, from mid to late Woodland into Iroquoian times, a pattern of behaviour was established. In the spring people moved into fishing camps; during summer the crops were sown and tended, while in the fall, crops were harvested, and the people fished. Hunting was a year round activity. Initially villages were small but as the intensity of agriculture grew, so did the population. By the time of first European contact, villages and their areas under cultivation were quite large. There were four main groups of Native Peoples at time of contact: Huron, Petun, Neutral, and St. Lawrence Iroquois. All grew crops, but the largest and best historical records

White Elm

(Ulmus americana)

Located in Nicolet Township, Algoma District, this tree has a diameter of 151 centimetres with a height of 37.5 metres.

(compiled from Champlain and French missionary priests) concern the Huron. During the very early 1600s, both Champlain and Father Sagard described much of the country we now call Huronia—roughly north Simcoe County—as "well cleared." Current estimates[2] of the native population at the time of Champlain's visit are 20–30,000 or more, a density of 2,400/km[2].

Villages were established on well-drained soils with a permanent source of water and a supply of timber for construction of longhouses. The average village covered 4 to 6 acres (1.5–2.5 hectares) with a population of about 1,000 persons; some villages were clustered by clans; all but the smallest settlements comprised two or more clans. Polewood (eastern white-cedar, tamarack or eastern white pine) used to form the frames for the longhouse, or to erect palisades around a village, came from immature stands. For a large village, it has been estimated that an area of 46 acres (18.5 hectares) of woodland and forested swamps was needed to provide the construction timbers.

When palisades were built, even more polewood was required. The village of Cahiagué, near Warminster, used 24,000 logs for the palisade alone (although this site may have had an unusually large number of logs of large size). At another site, the Draper[3] site (circa 1500 A.D.), mould diameters in the locations of palisade poles averaged 7.1 to 8.4 cm; the actual diameters of the poles would have been less; some 15,710 poles were used in the construction. Longhouse log diameters averaged 7.6 cm, and an estimated 13,680 poles were required for the walls; poles for the roofs and inside bench supports would be additional.

Trees were cut with polished stone axes, and it's estimated that a 7 inch diameter (18 cm) tree could be felled in 5 to 7 minutes. Longhouses were covered with elm bark which was obtained by girdling large trees in the Spring when the bark "slips" easily.

Corn, the main crop, was stored in bark casks placed in storage bins inside, at the ends of the longhouses. Average consumption of corn, the staple food all year, has been estimated at 1.3 lbs. (0.6 kg) per person per day, or 9 bushels per person per year. Sunflowers were used to provide hair oil. The Huron did not grow much tobacco; instead they obtained most of their needs in trade with the Petun to the west and south. Apparently the Huron were not great meat eaters; any game was eaten as killed and not stored, fish, however, was dried and smoked.

It was estimated that a village of 1,000 people required about

K. A. Armson

360 acres (145 hectares) in crops for subsistence. Heidenreich (1971) estimated that a population of 21,000, based on that consumption, would require 189,000 bushels a year, and that a cultivated area of 50,000 acres (20,243 hectares) would be required to grow that amount. A population of 21,000 is considerably less than Champlain's estimate of 30,000 for Huronia and significantly smaller than some current estimates. Yields of corn have been estimated at 27 bushels per acre (67 bushels per hectare) on the average, so that to produce 9,000 bushels for a village of 1,000, a minimum annual area of 333 acres (135 hectares) would be under cultivation.

Villages moved about every eight to twelve years, forced by decreasing crop yields due to lowered soil fertility, the increased distances women had to go to tend the crops, and lack of firewood. Usually the fields would be abandoned when corn yields only produced about eight bushels per acre (20 bushels per hectare). Distances of one and a half to two miles (2.4 to 3.2 km.) from a village were about the maximum that women would walk to tend crops.

The procedure for clearing crop land for use was very much a "hoe" culture, similar to the "slash and burn" practised in most subtropical areas today, except that, as far as we know, the Iroquois did not use fire to clear forests. Smaller trees would be felled and stripped of branches, which would be burned. Polewood stems suitable for construction of houses or palisades would be used for those purposes. Large trees were girdled. Apparently the Huron knew that the most effective time to girdle a tree was just after it had leafed out in early summer. The combination of ash from burnt branches and foliage, together with the

Photo courtesy Algonquin Provincial Park

exposure of the forest floor to sunlight and higher temperatures, lead to greater rates of decomposition and therefore increased nutrients and higher soil fertility. Corn was planted in these open areas. The Huron used a wooden stick which placed four to six corn seeds at a spacing of about one metre. Beans and squash were often planted along side the corn. The beneficial effect of the legume (beans) with its associated rhizobial, nitrogen-fixing bacteria, was recognized without knowing the reason. When the corn was about knee-high, the Huron piled earth up in a small hill around each set of plants; the same hills were used each year.

Given that coarser textured, well-drained soils were the primary soils used for crops, and Heidenreich's estimation that 50,000 acres (20,243 hectares) were required for cultivation at any one time, it appears a total of 157,861 acres (63,911 hectares) was suitable for cultivation in Huronia (essentially the present area of north Simcoe county). Thus the impact of Huron agriculture had a profound effect on the forest cover. Abandoned cultivated lands would revert to scrub vegetation, and ultimately forest regrowth.

The nature of cultivation, and its duration, determined the establishment of forest cover, which was either primarily from species immediately surrounding the area, or from isolated residuals within the area. Birches, some poplar, and conifers, mainly eastern white and some red pine, predominated on the coarser, well-drained soils. Maples and later successional species were more likely found on the finer textured soils.

Forests of broadleaved species would also be cleared when they were on coarser, well-drained soils. Today's Awenda Provincial Park was originally a forest predominantly of maple, beech and hemlock with subordinate birch, oak and pine—all of which was cleared about 1450 A.D. and put into crops by the Huron. This site, showed evidence of soil erosion for the next 200 years, which only declined after 1650 when there was no longer any Aboriginal occupation; erosion increased again following 1870, with the onset of clearing and settlement by Europeans.

Indian burial mounds, Serpents Mounds, Rice Lake

K. A. Armson

The picture that emerges for southern Ontario is generally that of large cleared areas under cultivation on the sandy moraines and outwash sands and loams, interspersed with forests on the finer textured and less well-drained soils which would largely be host to broadleaved trees and some conifers. This conclusion is reinforced by the historical observations of persons like Father Sagard who stated that he would, *"lose my way usually in these corn fields more often than in the meadows and forests."* Although much of what we know comes from studies of Huronia, crops were also being grown in eastern Ontario. In 1613 Champlain, when in the vicinity of present day Cobden, noted the sparsely planted corn and compared it to that of the Indians in Florida. When in Huronia, Champlain remarked on the large areas of "wild wheat and peas" and the lack of wood and amount of exhausted soils.

We know that red and eastern white pines would have been dominant species on the well-drained sandy soils as a result of natural disturbances, particularly fire. Pollen analyses in southern Ontario (Crawford Lake) show an increase in pine pollen following the disappearance of corn pollen. Thus, abandoned lands would support forest stands in various successional stages through to polewood. There is further evidence that there was reuse of lands for crops some 60 years after abandonment. Such reuse was probably widespread and would have made land clearing much easier.

Reconstructed Indian longhouse at Crawford Lake Conservation area. Note elm bark covering.

If Heidenreich's estimates are accurate, it means that, with few exceptions, mature and very old pine forests would be rare, although small groups of old trees could be present. Only after the virtual obliteration of the Huron by the Iroquois in the mid 1650s did these pine forests grow to older ages and larger sizes. Bowman (1979), who used the earliest records of surveyors of pine for mast timbers in the late 1790s as a starting point, was able to match up an area of even-aged pine forest to that which most probably could have been used for crops adjacent to a Huron village (Draper site) abandoned in 1550. From the sizes of the trees being considered for naval masts, it could be assumed that they were of the order of 150–200 years of age, which would fit well with their becoming established on abandoned fields. The area of pine forest was 7.8 km^2 (1,900 acres); this was not all a result of the Draper village, but also from the activities of other villages in the vicinity. The implications from these pieces of evidence, compiled from different locations in southern Ontario, suggest that many of the "virgin" and "pristine" forests, especially of pine, perceived by the early European settlers in the mid 1800s, had actually grown to mature and over-mature conditions on abandoned agricultural lands as a result of the decimation of the Aboriginal population 200 hundred years earlier. More recently, it has been postulated that cooler climatic conditions during the period of the Little Ice Age (1000 A.D.–1850 A.D.) also produced the vegetative changes that have been ascribed to revegetation of Aboriginal agricultural lands. Most probably, both factors, anthropogenic and climatic, separately or more likely in combination, resulted in the development of the forests viewed by the early European settlers.

The mythology associated with the common perception of pristine forests lives on, unrealistically warping the concept of "protection" of old growth forests.

K. A. Armson

1650 to 1850 Waterways and War

The decimation of Aboriginal populations by war and disease during the mid 1600s meant that much of southern Ontario reverted to forests in various stages of successional development. In the central and northern parts of the province, Algonquian families of Objibwa and Cree had little impact on the forests. Natural disturbances of wind, fire and insects maintained a forest pattern that continued well into the 19th and early 20th centuries. The rivers, lakes and streams were pathways for movement for both Native Peoples and the early explorers; these would continue to be used for the next two centuries by the military, settlers, forest industry, and others.

French trade routes were located primarily along the Ottawa River, across Lake Nipissing and on to the north shore of Lake Huron, thence north to Lake Superior and westwards, or alternatively along Lake Ontario, thence south through the Detroit or Niagara areas. Montréal was the hub of the French fur trade, and main locations of active trapping lay outside of southern Ontario. French and Indian fur trading extended into the northeast and northwest areas of northern Ontario. The Hudson Bay Company shared this territory and established trading posts in Hudson and James Bays after 1670.

The Treaty of Paris (1763), granted Britain possession of French Canada, and fur trading intensified. Main voyageur routes used the St. Lawrence and Ottawa rivers, then via portages, Lake Nipissing into Lakes Huron and Superior and west, or north to James and Hudson Bays. Throughout, Ontario's forests remained virtually untouched because human settlement was primarily in the regions of the lower St. Lawrence and the Maritimes.

With the onset of the American revolution, the Royal Navy, which had taken masting timbers from the New England colonies since 1652, moved north to Nova Scotia, New Brunswick and Québec for its supply. The area of Ontario remained unexploited for timber, although surveys for naval masting timbers were made along the north side of Lake Ontario in the late 1700s. Lumbering was still essentially confined to the lower St. Lawrence and eastwards.

By 1850 settlement had progressed along the water routes of the St. Lawrence, the north shore of Lake Ontario, Niagara Peninsula, the Grand and Thames rivers, and the Amherstburg – Lake St. Clair area (Figure 5-22); southeastern Ontario was more fully settled because of access provided by the Rideau canal. These locations reflected previous trade and fort locations, as well as the settlement by United Empire Loyalists and others, mainly Germans and pacifists, moving into Canada from the United States to escape the Revolutionary War. The new settlers tended to occupy the finer-textured soils dominated by tolerant hardwoods, knowing from previous experience that these soils would be the most fertile. During the period from the American Revolution to the War of

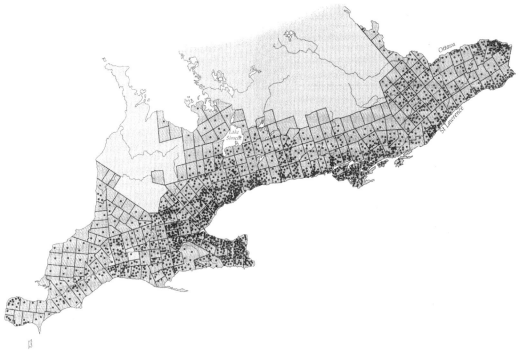

Figure 5-22

Main areas of cleared land in Upper Canada, 1842.

Source: Historical Atlas of Canada, Vol.II, Plate 14

K. A. Armson

1812, incursions in the forest were to clear land for agriculture and the production of timber for local building and firewood. Sawmills were small and water powered. Their lumber was primarily for local use—buildings and in many instances for access as plank roads.

The Napoleonic Wars in Europe dramatically changed the face of central and southern Ontario's forests. First, Britain had a high demand for pine timber, subsequently a demand from the United States continued in one form or another to the present as a major source of trade revenue to Ontario and Canada. Prior to the Napoleonic period, Britain relied on the Baltic countries for its softwood timber, which supply was threatened and then cut off by Napoleon in 1806. Shipments of timber from British North America more than doubled from 1807 to 1808, much of the wood in the form of squared timbers of eastern white and red pine.

A GLIMPSE OF FOREST AND STREAM.

On the Chaffey Road, north of Huntsville. August, 1875.

—By George Harlow White.

Octopus Tree

This peculiar-looking sugar maple has grown slowly on a rocky ridge in bush near the village of Bellrock. It has a profusion of large branches which form the lower stem; many of them bend into the earth and emerge a few metres away. Though not a tall tree (17 metres), its d.b.h. (diameter at breast height) is 117 centimetres and its crown spread 25 metres

Second, following the end of the European wars, the subsequent industrial revolution sent a wave of immigration from the United Kingdom to Canada in the 1800s, which resulted in massive movements of settlers into the forested areas of southern and lower central Ontario. Consequently, large amounts of forest lands were converted to agricultural use. During the late 1700s and into the first half of the 1800s, loggers and settlers confined their activities primarily along the waterways, although roads were also used to a limited extent. Initially, major incentives for road development were for military and defense purposes; only later would roads be viewed as providing access to forest lands for settlers.

The focus was on land, not forests; this was exemplified by the acquisition, through purchase or treaty, of virtually all the Aboriginal lands in southern and central Ontario by 1850 for purposes of settlement. The creation of the new province of Upper Canada in 1791, and the appointment of Colonel John Graves Simcoe as its first Lieutenant-Governor—known for his enthusiasm for promoting settlement—gave added impetus to agricultural settlement. This was not without its problems as large blocks of Ontario's land consisted of Crown and Clergy reserves (one seventh each of all lands). An entrenched group of senior military and government families were granted large land holdings, ostensibly in lieu of the otherwise inadequate salaries they received, *"far more land was held by Loyalists, the military and self-seeking officials than was received by settlers intending to make their home in Ontario County"*[6]. Many of the larger grants[7] were never cultivated. By 1824, eight million acres (3,237,556 hectares) had been granted of which less than 1,250,000 acres (505,868 hectares or 15.6 per cent) were granted to regular settlers. Five million acres (2,023,472 hectares or 62.5 per cent) were being held as speculation, and only 500,000 acres (20,235 hectares or 1.25 per cent) were under cultivation.

The War of 1812 with the United States, and increasing discontent within both Upper and Lower Canada with the system of favouritism of the privileged classes culminating in the rebellion of 1837, dampened to some degree the rate of colonization of Ontario's forest lands. Further, grants of lands brought no revenues to the Crown and although timber, especially pine was reserved to the Crown on granted lands as well as Crown lands, there was no systematic or effective means of enforcing regulations about its cutting or receiving payment.

K. A. Armson

Efforts to remedy this came with the appointment of Peter Robinson as the Commissioner of Crown lands and Surveyor General of Woods and Forests in 1827. Crown lands were to be sold by public auction and cutting of Crown timber on Crown lands would be by licences, also disposed of by public auction. Timber was to be cut within nine months of the issue of the licence; each licence was for no more than 2,000 cubic feet, and payment for timber cut was to be within 15 months of the licence issue.

Scalers[8] were appointed in the various districts in order to ensure proper measurement of timber. In 1826, dues per cubic foot were highest for oak at 1.5 pence, red pine was 1 penny and eastern white pine a halfpenny. Dues were doubled on logs which would not square more than 8 inches. Thus the incentive was to cut large timbers for the square timber trade with Britain.

Photo courtesy Algonquin Provincial Park

This established a pattern of culling forest stands for the largest and straightest trees, which resulted in partial cutting of many pine stands and the creation of more favourable conditions for establishment of broadleaved species. When fire followed logging in these situations, depending on severity and timing—both in terms of season and seed crop—a new pine forest could be regenerated which would provide timber for the forest industry in the 1900s.

Ontario's first raft of square timber left Ottawa in 1806 but by 1815 there was still only one sawmill in the Ottawa district. The timber trade burgeoned in the 1840s, and by 1845, 27 million cubic feet were rafted to Québec City for export, mainly to Britain.

The end of the Napoleonic wars, brought massive immigration from the British Isles, especially of Scots and Irish and former military persons who received grants of land for settlement. In 1820, 2,000 Scots, mainly weavers, settled in the area of Perth, south of Ottawa. In 1825, 2,000 Irish settled north of Rice Lake in what would become Peterborough (named for Peter Robinson).

Schemes for settlement, such as that of the Canada Land Company for over a million acres (400,000 + hectares) in western Ontario, and the major clearing along the north shore of Lake Erie by Colonel Thomas Talbot's settlers, resulted in wholesale clearing and burning of forests for farming. Major transportation routes remained waterways but with settlement being taken up on the fronts of Lakes Ontario and Erie, overland access became increasingly necessary. Three main roads were constructed, primarily for military purposes—Dundas Street from Burlington to the Thames River (London), Yonge Street from York (Toronto) to Lake Simcoe,

How wood is measured, or let me count the ways

Timber exported to Great Britain was measured in *'loads'* (1 load=50 cubic feet). Initially as *square timber,* then as *deals, planks* and *boards*. *Waney timber* was essentially square timber from the lower bole of the pine tree with the edges rounded or bevelled and was of high quality. Deals and planks were sawn products more than 3 inches (7.6 cm) thick and of varying widths and lengths; boards were less than 2 inches (4.8 cm) thick. Oak *staves* were a major export from southwestern Ontario after the opening of the Welland canal. With the shift in timber, exports to the United States, initially as logs rafted across the Great Lakes, then as sawn timber the measure used was the *board foot* which is one foot (30 cm) by one foot and one inch (2.54 cm) thick. Stumpage (price paid to the owner of the log or tree prior to processing) is based on the volume of wood. Thus for sawlogs various 'rules' have been developed to provide estimates of board foot volumes. The Scribner Log rule and the Doyle Log rule were used in Ontario, the latter as the official rule until 1952 when it was replaced by the Ontario Rule. Different rules give different values and thus owners often will specify the rule to be used. A *standard* was used to describe a log of 200 board feet. Since 1981 all Crown timber is measured in *cubic metres*. Fuelwood and pulpwood have been traditionally measured in *cords* (1 cord = 128 cubic feet of solid wood and air spaces). When the bark is left on, a cord is considered to contain 85 cubic feet of solid wood, or if peeled (bark removed) 100 cubic feet. Prior to the use of metric units pulpwood was often measured as *cunits* (100 cubic feet of solid wood). Wood chips used for pulp are measured in metric tonnes (1,000 kg).

K. A. Armson

and the road along the northshore of Lake Ontario from York to Kingston and then to Montréal. Yonge Street opened up the area directly north of York and, together with the completion of the Penetanguishene road in 1814, provided a link to the Georgian Bay. The completion of the Rideau canal in 1832 provided access in eastern Ontario and a means of moving lumber from eastern Ontario along the Rideau to Kingston where it was shipped across Lake Ontario to Oswego before being moved into the Erie canal (which opened in 1825). Road access, generally, was poor to non-existent.

Many of the settlers from Great Britain had little or no knowledge of farming; in addition, the cash market for their crops was limited. Initially the main cash product was often the ash they collected from burning timber, particularly hardwoods, to clear their lands. The ash was taken to local "potasheries" where it was leached and the residue dried for sale to the British textile and pottery industries.

Photo courtesy Algonquin Provincial Park

When settlers received land grants, they were required to meet certain conditions as to the area to be cleared, the erection of a building (16 feet by 20 feet in area, approximately 5m by 6m), and clearance of one half the road allowance in front of their properties. Such roads, needless to say, were of uneven and low quality. Often much of the road would be corduroyed with poles in low areas or (after the advent of mills) surfaced with planks.

Wheat was the main crop, along with oats and barley. Little attention was paid to soil fertility, and settlers would be forced to clear more land every eight to ten years. Land which had been "farmed out" would become rough pasture at best.

This pattern of land exploitation at ever increasing distances by settlers has its parallel in the logging patterns of northern Ontario, which continued well into the mid 1900s, when mills would cut the closest wood first. As roads were opened north from Lake Ontario in the 1830s and 1840s, and local grist and sawmills were established, opportunities for the transport and sale of lumber

Bur Oak

(Quercus macrocarpa)

Located in Burford Township, Brant County, this tree has a diameter of 212 centimetres with a height of 29.3 metres.

and fuelwood to the larger centres such as Toronto increased.

In 1837–38, the Scugog River was dammed at Lindsay to create a larger Lake Scugog, which provided a means to raft timber from Victoria County down to Port Perry where newly established steam sawmills cut it into lumber which was then shipped down a plank road to Whitby to be sold or shipped across Lake Ontario to Oswego. Building dams on streams and rivers to facilitate the transportation of sawlogs was common, and left a legacy of water-bodies that are now used primarily for recreation.

During the late 1800s, railways began to supplant roads as the main means of transporting goods and people. The Toronto and Nipissing railway supplied cordwood to the city, and concern at that time over price-fixing of the fuelwood supply brings eerie echoes to those with similar concerns about gasoline prices today. It was not only the clearing of forests for agriculture and timber that transformed Ontario's forests, but the cutting of fuelwood for the stoves of the townsfolk and farmers.

In his report of 1886, R.W. Phipps, Clerk of Forestry reported a survey from 160 townships in 17 counties on the amount of fire-wood available in standing woodlots. Only seven of the counties noted extensive use of coal replacing firewood, often due to the latter's unavailability. The forests of eastern, central and south-western Ontario which existed on well-drained soils began to disappear, to be replaced by arable lands, pasture, and abandoned wastelands. This was an accelerating process, one that would reach its peak in the next 70 years.

As the 1840s drew to a close, major changes were made in the regulations accessing timber on Crown lands. The Act of Union, in 1841, reunited the two provinces of Upper and Lower Canada. The Crown Timber Act of 1849 set out the framework for disposition of timber on Crown lands; its specifications, with some modifications persist to this day.

K. A. Armson

1851 to 1920 Lumber, Newsprint and the beginnings of Conservation

Settlement accelerated into central Ontario as the province opened up opportunities for lumbering on Crown lands. War and its aftermath continued to be a major factor affecting both the timber industry and the rate of agricultural settlement: the Crimean War (1853–1854) impacted on the flow of Russian timber to Britain, while the American Civil War (1861–1865) and its subsequent reconstruction period provided impetus to the industry.

There was an increasing flow of immigrants from Great Britain. The Elgin-Marcy Treaty (Reciprocity Treaty of 1854) reduced tariffs on products imported between Canada and the United States. Exports of timber to the United States increased, while exports to Great Britain, although greater, diminished. Development of the lumber industry was linked to the opening up of forest lands. Logging required men, animals—horses and oxen—these in turn required food which farming communities on adjacent agricultural lands could provide. The forestry industry was also recognized as a significant source of revenue to the country. In 1866, Sir Alex Campbell, in his annual report, noted that the value of timber exports was $73,004,312 between 1856 and 1863, as compared with $16,765,981 for agricultural products. Great Britain was still the major recipient of timber exports compared to the United States, at a ratio of approximately 3:1.

Concerns were also being expressed over what happened to logged-over lands which often burnt, as well as the increasing amounts of wasteland resulting from initial clearing by settlers who

Comparing the state of Ontario's forest lands over time—a case of *apples & oranges*

Systematic, periodic surveys, using consistent measures on the same forest land units are the only way changes can be reliably identified. Unfortunately, none of these criteria have applied in Ontario. As noted in Table 5-1 the data in 1896 came from assessment rolls only for counties in southern Ontario. The first published provincial forest survey* did not include southern Ontario and included data from a variety of sources. The provincial inventories published in 1963 and those of 1986 and 1996 used different methodologies and geographic extent. Those of 1986 and 1996 are essentially comparable although the individual management units to which they apply are sometimes different. Further, as with all survey data, it is out-of-date the moment it is obtained. In Ontario the cycle used for forest surveys is 20 years; for the 1996 survey the data are between 5 to 10 years old.

* Sharpe, J.F. and J.A. Brodie. 1931 The Forest Resources of Ontario 1930. Forestry Branch, Ontario Department of Lands & Forests, Toronto. p. 60 + maps.

would later abandon their cultivated acreage. In 1864, a select committee was established to *"enquire into causes of the rapid destruction of our forests and the means to be adopted to prevent it. To consider the expediency of reserving as forests, the extensive tracts of land which abound with exportable timber but are unsuitable for cultivation; of enacting a forest law, and to suggest that system which in it's opinion is best adapted to the requirements and conditions of the country."* The committee never published its report. Political upheaval associated with the proposed Canadian Confederation interfered. It is interesting to note that the terms of reference in the report contain the notion of land use designation, the separation of timber from agricultural allocation, and the use of forest land reserves as sources of revenue in the form of exportable timber.

Fish and wildlife populations were undergoing changes during this same period of forest exploitation and the clearing of lands for settlement. Habitats were destroyed as hunting and fishing were essentially uncontrolled. The cougar, which occupied much the same territory in southern Ontario as the white-tailed deer, became "extinct" sometime in the late 1800s. Wild turkey, which had been an inhabitant primarily of the oak-beech-maple forests since the days of the early Native Peoples, was reduced in numbers until it virtually disappeared about 1900. This species began to be reintroduced in Ontario in the 1960s and today there is a population large enough to support regulated hunting of these birds. This fact speaks much to the renewed presence of adequate forest habitats in southern Ontario for the turkey and other threatened species. The abundance of the Ontario salmon, which was a staple for both Native Peoples and the early settlers along the "old Ontario strand," has been portrayed in print and pictures, but by 1850, salmon runs in streams had declined calamitously. One such stream flowed through the farmland of Samuel Wilmot, who, on his own initiative, established the first government fish hatchery in North America in 1866[9]. In southwestern Ontario, the destruction of the prairie-savannah conditions resulted in the loss or significant reduction of fauna and flora associated with these types. Today, this is another example of a habitat type which is now being recreated.

Non-human disturbances, most likely, were the key factors affecting wildlife populations in northern Ontario coupled with hunting and trapping pressures that were undoubtedly synergistic (for either habitat or disease related causes). In northwestern

118

K. A. Armson

Ontario the history[10] of a migratory species like the woodland caribou indicates that its population reached a temporary low in the 1820–1840 period—the 1830s 'ungulate drought'—before any significant development activity by Europeans. The building of the railway through this area from the 1870s to early 1880s, and subsequent logging associated with sawmills in the late 1800s (pulp and paper mills in the early 1900s), and agricultural development in Dryden and Rainy River not only changed the forest habitat, but disrupted the caribou migration routes. Furthermore, cutovers resulting from logging, coupled with natural regeneration after wildfires, provided major opportunities for the growth of white-tailed deer and thus increased exposure to the parasitic brainworm, as well as increased predation.

By the mid nineteenth century, large-scale clearing of lands in southern Ontario could no longer accommodate the increasing influx of immigrants. In 1868, Ontario's Free Grants and Homestead Act opened up the districts of Parry Sound and Muskoka and other areas to settlers. This move was also accompanied by increased sale of timber on Crown lands to the sawmilling industry. Much of the land being offered up in this Act was on the Canadian Shield, and was totally unsuitable for agriculture; further, settlers were removed from the relatively accessible agricultural markets existing in southern Ontario. Inevitably, these new landowners turned to logging, working for sawmillers, or cutting and selling pine to the sawmillers from their own lands to add to the meagre income they might receive from farm crops.

Concern in southern Ontario for the extent of the so-called "wastelands" was growing within farming communities. An 1896 survey of 35 of the 42 counties (Essex, Kent, Elgin, Norfolk, Haldimand, Welland and Hastings were omitted) based on township assessors' returns indicated a large area of wasteland (Table 5-1).

The clearing of these "inferior lands for agriculture" caused R.W.Phipps as Clerk of Forestry in 1883 to lament, *"pressure of poverty was sometimes severe, and men sometimes driven almost to the starving point had little scruple in destroying 100 dollars worth of timber to procure five dollars worth of wheat, when they could get the five dollars, could not get the hundred then and were by no means sure they ever would."*

Photo courtesy Algonquin Provincial Park

Table 5-1 Changes in forested lands 1896 to 1996
Summaries of Forested and Non-Forested Lands in southern Ontario
—1996,[11] 1963[12], 1896[13].All areas converted to hectares

1996 Forest Inventory			
Total	**Productive*** **Forest Land**	**Non-Productive**** **Forest land. "Waste lands"** **of 1897 report**	**Non-Forested***** **Land**
7,473,632	2,076,121 27.8%	188,620 2.5%	5,208,891 69.7%

1963 Forest Inventory			
9,311,600	2,344,400 25.2%	483,200 5.2%	6,484,00 69.6%

1896 Forest Inventory			
6,029,559	1,263,055 20.9%	948,864 15.7%	3,867,640 63.3%

*   lands bearing or capable of bearing commercial timber

**   lands not capable of bearing commercial timber because of low productivity, e.g. open and treed muskeg, brush and alder covered lands, rock

*** lands permanently withdrawn from forest use, e.g. agricultural lands, cities, towns and villages, roads, power lines etc.

In order to provide some comparisons, data from provincial forest inventories for 1963 and 1996 are also given. Two features of the data in this table be must emphasized: first, the determining basis for each set is different; second, the areas are not the same although they largely cover southern Ontario. The area of the 1996 data is closest to the counties assessed in 1897, while the 1963 data included areas to the north of the former two. The 1896 information was taken from assessors' reports and undoubtedly the numbers for "cleared" which are in the "non-forested" category are conservative; as an assessor put it, *the farmers all try to return to the assessor as small a clearance as they can, to keep down taxation....*[14] Despite these discrepancies, the data do provide an insight into the trends in forest land over the past century and a half.

Figure 5-23
Cleared land in the Trent Valley watershed.

Photo from Commission of Conservation, 1912

The major depletion of southern Ontario's forests was probably complete by 1900. [Although not strictly comparable, the Ontario Royal Commission on Forestry in 1947 cited the proportion of woodland in southern Ontario to be 9.7 per cent in 1943.] Since 1900 and particularly since 1943, woodland has increased partly due to natural regeneration of abandoned lands, but more particularly as a result of government reforestation programs during the 1900s. Note that the proportion of non-forested land (Table 5-1) has remained relatively constant. The expansion of cities and towns has been primarily at the expense of agricultural land areas, although this does not mean that there have not been major forest land reductions in local or regional areas. Although no data is available for Essex, Kent and Norfolk counties for 1896, the 1963 data for the area of Essex, Kent and Lambton counties gives the proportion of productive and non-productive forest lands as 8.4 per cent; recent information for Essex and Kent counties shows it as less than 3 per cent. 1978 data on Ontario's woodland cover for Counties and Regional Municipalities is presented in Larson et al, 1999[15].

One of the first detailed forest inventories in Ontario was undertaken in the 30 townships forming the watershed of the Trent River north of Lindsay. The reason for the survey, conducted in 1912, was concern over the water supply for the Trent Canal

Figure 5-24

Annual harvest of eastern white and red pine sawlogs from Ontario Crown forests.

Source: P.L.Aird, 1985. In Praise of Pine. Inf.Rep. PI–X–52, Canadian Forest Service, Ottawa

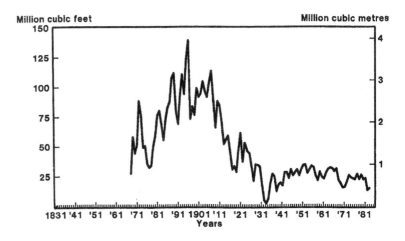

K. A. Armson

because of the extensive logging, clearing, and fires in the area. It is of particular interest because 20 of the 30 townships in the survey are in the Minden Crown Management Unit (now a Sustainable Forest Licence unit) for which there is recent (1996) forest information. In 1912, cleared land amounted to 11 per cent, whereas now it is 4 per cent; the proportion of forest land was 87 per cent in 1912 and has increased to 91 per cent at present. This is largely attributable to the reforestation of formerly cleared lands. The nature of the forest has changed as a result of logging, first for pine and then, beginning in the early 1900s, hardwoods, mainly clearcut, over several townships for chemical wood distillation. The changes in Minden Crown Management Area are typical for much of the Great Lakes – St. Lawrence region. Some local variation occurs because of the intensities and frequencies of disturbances both human and non-human, the physiographic features of a particular forest, and changes in land uses and ownership, although the latter does not normally affect the general pattern.

The nature of the forests before and after disturbance for the period from first exploitation into the early 1900s is presented in Tables 5-2 a, b, c.

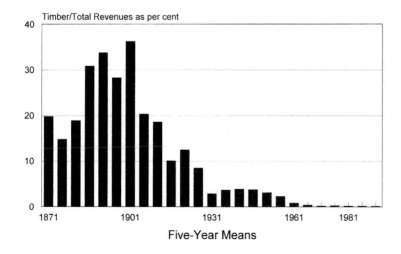

Figure 5-25
Timber revenues as per cent of total Ontario government revenues, 1867–1990
Source: Pross, A.P., 1967 & Ontario Gov.

Table 5-2a
General Pattern of Forest Types in the Great Lakes – St. Lawrence Region
following Logging and other Disturbances, 1800s to early 1900s

Before Logging or Clearing Pine Forests	Result of Logging or other Disturbance	Resultant Forest Type
Eastern white and red pines on well-drained deep sands; little hardwoods except some aspen poplars and white birch; stands of wildfire origin, even-aged.	In the early days for square timber, only large trees were taken, leaving trees for natural seeding; fires in these logged areas consumed much of the residual slash and provided seed beds for pines. As logging moved to saw timber the utilization increased. Fires often followed the logging. Clearing for agriculture on sandy soils was often followed by their abandonment	Even-aged stands with higher proportion of eastern white pine than red pine, compared to before logging, but with residual older pines in various stages of over-maturity. Given the availability of pine seed from adjacent stands or individual trees and occurrence of fire, an even-aged forest would be established. When seed sources were not present and fire did not occur, although individual pines might develop, the forest enters a brush i.e. poplar/birch succession. This succession was also common on the abandoned farm lands
Eastern white and red pines on shallow tills over bedrock or fractured bedrock; considerable component of hardwoods—aspen poplars, sugar maple and yellow birch on tills; red oak and red maple on fractured bedrock; even-aged, although on fractured bedrock some variability in age classes.	Logging for large trees did not leave large openings in the forest, on till sites. Tree sizes on bedrock were often too small or, if large, not easily accessible. Fire after logging highly variable and often repeated	On till sites, usually a hardwood stand dominated by poplar, with white birch, sugar maple, white ash, balsam fir, and variable amounts of even-aged eastern white pine: on northerly and moist sites, yellow birch, basswood and hemlock are common: on fractured bedrock, eastern white pine with red oak and red maple.
Jack pine on deep well-drained sands or on fractured bedrock: almost pure stands with little to no hardwoods: even-aged on deep sands, but on fractured bedrock often open-grown stands of varying ages: wildfire origin	Little logged in the 1800s and early 1900s, except for local use or construction of railroads. Residual smaller trees left and usually areas burnt after logging	Even-aged stands of jack pine, and depending on the intensity of the fire, higher content of aspen poplars and white birch the lower the intensity of fire

Table 5-2b
General Pattern of Forest Types in the Great Lakes – St. Lawrence Region
following Logging and other Disturbances, 1800s to early 1900s

Before Logging or Clearing Broadleaved Forests	Result of Logging or other Disturbance	Resultant Forest Type
Sugar maple-beech forests on deep tills sometimes with scattered eastern white pine trees and other hardwoods such as white ash, yellow birch, basswood, and black cherry: major disturbances are infrequent fires—often ground fires—and windthrows: stands usually a mosaic of age classes.	Initially logging did not occur with any intensity except for clearcutting for firewood. In two areas, Haliburton and South River, clearcutting for chemical wood began in the early 1900s. Logging (high grading) for quality saw and veneer logs in the 1900s did not begin until the 1920s: where accessible, large pine were removed: infrequent ground fires and windthrow have been continuing disturbances.	After clearcutting, mixed hardwoods with some sugar maple but also yellow birch, white ash, basswood, black cherry were common results. With highgrading, the main result was lower quality trees predominantly sugar maple. In local openings caused by disturbance, mainly after fire and windthrow, depending on the local site conditions a variety of small stands would develop, often groups of eastern hemlock and yellow birch on the moister soils. Where disturbance was severe, poplar and white birch and red oak and white ash were common types.
Aspen poplar, white birch often with a mixture of balsam fir on well-drained sands, shallow tills, and (for white birch) talus slopes: successional stands after major wildfires: even-aged	Normally not logged, but cleared for other uses	Successional forests in which the poplars and white birch, as they deteriorate and die, are replaced by understory species such as balsam and other conifers and maples.

K. A. Armson

Table 5-2c

General Pattern of Forest Types in the Great Lakes – St. Lawrence Region following
Logging and other Disturbances, 1800s to early 1900s

Before Logging or Clearing Other Conifers	Result of Logging or other Disturbance	Resultant Forest Type
Hemlock occurred in relatively pure stands which seeded in after wildfire, or as components of hardwood stands usually in association with yellow birch.	Hemlock was not generally logged but trees in many stands were girdled for their bark which was used for its tannin.	Stands which were girdled became invaded by hardwoods; stands not girdled remained until a major fire or windthrow occurred when, depending on the magnitude and severity of the disturbance, a new stand with varying hemlock: hardwood ratios would establish.
Eastern white-cedar was mainly in pure stands on poorly drained soils adjacent to streams, or scattered along stream sides. Some occurrence on upland soils in mixtures with poplar, white birch, white spruce and eastern white pine	Cedar stands were logged for poles and posts as well as being used for corduroying roads.	Cedar did not regenerate well after logging; instead it was replaced by black ash and balsam fir; cedar colonized abandoned cleared lands that had been used for pasture; on the upland soils it was replaced by poplar and balsam fir.
Tamarack occurred either as scattered individuals on poorly drained soils or in pure stands, the latter usually following a major disturbance	Apart from some local uses, because the timber is resistant to decay, no major logging occurred.	Tamarack regenerates naturally on the poorly-drained soils where it occurs; when a seed source is available, it will also regenerate well on upland soils to form pure stands, but as they mature the tamarack are replaced by hardwoods

By 1896 in the area stretching from Algoma in the west, through Parry Sound, Muskoka, to the Ottawa valley, 107 townships had been laid out for free grants. 25,000 people had settled on 3 million acres (1.2 million hectares). The dominating feature of the area was the logging of pine for the lumber industry; by the beginning of the 20th century, this supply was rapidly diminishing. Figure 5-24 shows both the rapid increase from the time of Confederation to the late 1880s and the subsequent drop. Not only was the export of lumber to Great Britain and the United States significant to Canada's balance of trade (and more importantly for Ontario's), revenues derived from the Crown charges paid by lumbermen to the province (Figure 5-25) were a major source of capital with which to provide the infrastructure of roads, schools and other amenities for southern areas of the province.

White Oak

(Quercus alba)

Located in Otonabe Township,

Peterborough County, this tree

has a diameter of 191

centimetres with a height of

27.1 metres.

Large-scale human disturbance of the northern forests in both the east and west did not occur until railway access. Lumbering in the Thunder Bay, and particularly Fort Frances and Rainy River areas for eastern white and red pines (which have been found in the northwestern range of the Great Lakes – St. Lawrence forest region) was limited except for markets in the midwest United States. Most settlement was concentrated in the Algoma-Sault Ste. Marie areas, and even this was minimal. By 1871 just 10,430 acres (4221 hectares) were cleared for agriculture in northwestern Ontario and of these, only 25 per cent were arable or improved pasture lands[16]. Much of the early exploration and surveys of northwestern Ontario was linked to mineral resources rather than timber.

There were authorized sales of timber on Crown lands in northwestern Ontario as early as 1872, but it was not until after 1885 that any major grants were made west of Sault Ste. Marie. The fact that most of the forests of the northwest were of fire origin is borne out by surveyors' reports. Alexander Niven surveyed the line between the districts of Thunder Bay and Rainy River in 1890 and stated, *"the country along the whole line has been burned at various times from seventy years down to seven years ago."*[17]

Although lumber was transported by water during this early period, it would be the railway that made possible the development of Northern Ontario's pulp and paper industry. And, although access by railway was a key, the door to Ontario's forest resources would not have been opened without the convergence of other features. The actual 'push' for railways was both political and commercially motivated, whether it was building of national lines—Canadian Pacific and Grand Trunk Pacific railways, or provincial lines—Algoma and Hudson Bay (ACR) and Temiskaming and Northern Ontario (TNO) railways.

Ontario wanted to develop new agricultural areas. The only place left was northern Ontario. The province wanted more immigrants from Great Britain and Europe, and there also was concern about the emigration of young people from southern Ontario farms, to western Canada at a time when the Ontario government would prefer them to remain within the province.

Although the lumbering of eastern white and red pine was generally declining, there was a burgeoning market for paper, especially newsprint, in the United States. Up until the mid to late 1880s, paper had been made from rags, but a number of new developments following rapidly one upon another, provided the

K. A. Armson

ability to make paper from wood fibres (groundwood pulp), and wood fibres treated with various sulphuric acid compounds (sulphite and sulphate pulps). White and black spruce were the main tree species used—black was preferred because of its longer fibres which gave greater strength to paper made from groundwood pulp. Balsam fir was another favourite source of wood fibre. The power requirements to grind wood, whether for groundwood or for subsequent treatment as chemical pulp were great, and the location of any pulp mill hinged on a local hydro-electric power supply. The first paper mill in Upper Canada, was located in Ancaster, and used rags for its raw material. In 1888, a mill in Georgetown was the first to use wood fibre for pulp production, utilizing electrical power from a generator on the Credit River.

In 1890, engineer and promoter, Francis H. Clergue, saw Sault Ste. Marie as the ideal location for a pulp mill. The city had already begun construction of a hydro-electric plant; there was a copious supply of water, and ready access by land, rail and water to the United States. By 1892, Clergue concluded an agreement with the province to provide a pulp mill, which was completed on schedule in 1895. He received a 21-year licence for the rights to log spruce, poplar, tamarack and jack pine over a huge area extending north of Sault Ste. Marie back from the shores of Lake Superior. Clergue's was the first mill in northern Ontario. Today, a paper mill still operates on the same site, more than a hundred years later—an example of the sustainability of forests, industry and community that has been little recognized.

Clergue was also responsible for the development of the steel industry, and owned an iron ore mine at Wawa. Although he could ship the ore out by boat, Clergue preferred to have land access and he negotiated with the province and federal government to build the Algoma Central Railway. The Canadian government provided a financial grant; the province offered a grant of 7,400 acres of Crown land with timber and mineral rights per mile of railway (1,872 km. per kilometre). During the 20th century these private lands became a rich source of timber for wood-using industries and, towards the end of the century, a major area for cottaging and recreation.

The Canadian Pacific Railway was completed between Winnipeg and the Lakehead in 1881. One result was a building boom in Winnipeg. Pine lumber from the Georgian Bay area—Simcoe County and Parry Sound—had a burgeoning western market. which also stimulated logging and sawmill development in

Making pulp from wood

A German, Keller, invented a process for making pulp by grinding logs in 1840. However, quite independently, it was a Nova Scotian, Charles Fenerty, who first made pulp by grinding spruce logs in 1841, although he didn't make it public until 1844. In 1867, an American, Tilghman, found that sulphurous acid would separate fibres in wood and laid the foundation for chemical pulping processes.

Walnut

(Black Walnut—juglans nigra)
Located north of Highway 2,
west of Cartaraqui, this tree
has a diameter of 180
centimetres with a height of
27.4 metres.

northwestern Ontario, particularly in the Fort Frances-Rainy River, and Kenora areas.

Since Confederation in 1867, Ontario had been disputing ownership of lands and resources in the northwestern areas of the province with the federal government. As a result, some lumber companies obtained their licences from the Dominion Lands Branch in Ottawa, at the same time the province was granting timber licences. This confusing state was settled in 1899 when, after an agreement between the two governments, Ontario cancelled all federal licences.

Markets for lumber, sawlogs, and for the newly developing pulp and paper industry, were primarily in the United States. In 1897 the United States, acting under a wave of protectionism, introduced the Dingley tariff which allowed the free importation of sawlogs, but placed a prohibitive duty on manufactured products. This posed a dilemma for both Ottawa and Ontario. Many companies in central and eastern Ontario had a profitable trade in sawlogs with the Americans and would not be affected. Other sawmills, especially those in the northwest, were looking to building up their businesses in lumber and expected the federal and provincial governments to react. Ottawa was reluctant to respond, but, in 1898, Ontario passed legislation requiring all pine logs cut from Ontario's Crown lands to be manufactured in Canada. This condition was later extended to pulpwood. By 1900, all wood from Crown lands had to be processed in Canadian mills, although provision was made for ministerial discretionary power to permit the export of logs under special circumstances. Ontario is the only province which allows the free movement of logs from provincial Crown lands to mills in other provinces; other provinces prohibit such movement from their Crown lands unless specially exempted.

The new manufacturing requirement meant that American capital flowed into Ontario and with a resultant boom in sawmill construction and productivity, particularly for eastern white and red pines. The reason for this apparent contradiction was that the Dingley tariff had included lumber largely as a result of lobbying by Michigan lumbermen who obtained their logs from Ontario and were opposed to the development of Ontario sawmills. The Ontario manufacturing requirement, however, meant that Michigan lumbermen could only meet their lumber supply requirements by opening mills in Ontario, with the resultant closing of mills in Michigan[18]. This is why there was a dramatic reduction, followed

K. A. Armson

by a rapid increase in pine sawlog volumes over this period as shown in Figure 5-24.

Opening of the north came with the completion of the Canadian Pacific Railway link from Winnipeg through the Lakehead to Montréal in 1885. Rail links from Kenora south to Fort Frances and International Falls, across the river, together with the building of the Temiskaming and Northern Ontario Railway from North Bay to Cochrane (where it linked to the east-west Grand Trunk Pacific Railway in 1908), provided further access. Ontario's northland, with its predominantly spruce and pine forests, replete with water for power and industrial purposes, was now laced with a net of railways.

To the south, the eastern, and midwestern United States, demand for newsprint was growing, and the supply of spruce pulpwood for newsprint from the American northeast could not keep up. In 1891, the McKinley tariff imposed a 15 per cent *ad valorem* duty on Canadian pulp and paper imported into the United States. American publishers looked into Ontario and assessed the rich source of raw material. They took political action, and the duty on Canadian pulp and paper was eliminated in 1913. The result was a flurry of investment in Ontario, with mills being built in Dryden(1913), Fort Frances(1914), Iroquois Falls (1917), Kapuskasing(1917), Kenora (1917), and Thunder Bay (1917). By 1928 there were 13 pulp mills operating in Ontario, drawing wood from Crown forest lands. Eight were in northwestern Ontario and five in the central and northeast. The Ontario Paper Company mill built at Thorold, in 1913 to supply newsprint to the *Chicago Tribune* had no Crown licensed lands, and relied on purchased wood.

The Canadian railway net also facilitated the influx of settlers for agricultural development. Ontario's politicians were dedicated to the notion that agricultural settlement was the key to the province's future. Because the clay soils in southern Ontario were so productive, they believed the same would hold true for the north. If the politicians had learned any lesson, it was that sandy soils could rapidly become "waste" lands. The link between the forest industry and settlement was clear, as Sir William Logan had noted in 1845, *"...the occupations of the lumberer and the farmer have been a great encouragement to each other...."* Dr. Bernhard Fernow, Dean of the Faculty of Forestry, University of Toronto, traversed the Grand Trunk Railway for 200 miles (320 km.) east and west of Cochrane, noting[19] that only 10–15 per cent of the area

Photo courtesy Algonquin Provincial Park

MEASUREMENT RULES

Log Rule—a formula to estimate the volume (usually in board feet) of lumber that may be sawed from logs of different sizes under various assumed conditions given their length and scaling (small end) diameter.

Doyle Rule—a log rule used in Eastern and Southern North America, particularly for hardwoods; the formula is

$$V = \left(\frac{D-4}{4}\right)^2 L$$

V = board foot volume
D = diameter inside bark at the small end in inches
L = length in feet

Note—the Doyle rule underestimates board foot volume in small logs and overestimates in large logs.

was *"first class for logging"* (meaning saw logs), and 35–50 per cent was in small-sized pulpwood, mainly black spruce. Fernow recognized on some parts of the area, *"the outlook for agriculture is undoubtedly bright,"* although he saw hay as a main crop!

Settlers flowed to Fort Frances-Rainy River, Cochrane, Dryden, Kapuskasing, Smooth Rock Falls, New Liskeard and the "little clay belt," Matheson and Iroquois Falls. It was not only the new pulp and paper mills which became symbiotic partners in the economic and social development of these forested lands, prospecting and mining in both northeastern and northwestern Ontario provided further incentives for development.

Discharged soldiers received land grants following the end of the Boer War in 1902 and in 1919 after World War I. Many of these 'Vet Lots'. were never taken up and cleared, remaining in forest until today. Others have been sold for their timber value.

The first two decades of the 20th century saw the development of a community infrastructure which continues to this day. The forest industry wanted black and white spruce trees for their mills, and for the most part it was the pulp and paper industry that characterized the north, not the sawmilling. True, there were a few large sawmills, but these were concentrated in the northwest, associated with eastern white and red pines.

Wildfires were a concern during the early pine logging period; most fires resulted from the clearing of land by settlers. Fires which occurred after logging were believed to be the reason why lands did not regenerate back to pine.

In 1898 a Royal Commission on Forestry, chaired by prominent lumberman, E.W.Rathbun, was instructed, *"To investigate and report on the subject of restoring and preserving the growth of white pine and other timber trees upon lands in the Province which are not adapted for agricultural purposes."* The Commission visited forests from the Trent River to Georgian Bay and north to the Lakehead and Rainy River, delivering its report in 1899 (although by then its title[20] had changed). The Commission's preliminary report, recommended that the fire ranging system inaugurated in 1886 be extended, but the main body of its report dealt with the dynamics of forest succession and forest ecology in a surprisingly knowledgeable manner. The Commission understood the role that forests and the forestry industry could play in Ontario: *"Important as trees are in the urban and rural parts, this importance is lost sight of when considering the far greater necessity of restoring a*

K. A. Armson

forest growth of desirable trees to large districts of the Province from which fire has removed the original forest and where land is unsuitable for agriculture. Herein lies the real question of Canadian forestry; what should be our proper course in utilizing forest products and in preserving the productive power of our forests." The Commission also studied the densely settled areas of southern Ontario, in their deliberations, arguing that southern Ontario should have a 25 per cent tree cover. [Table 5-1 shows present productive forest at 27 per cent.]

It is true that public concern about a natural resource usually does not become crystallized until the resource is threatened or destroyed. The settlement and excessive exploitation of forest lands in Ontario, and the northeastern part of the continent, had, by the latter part of the 19th century, created conditions which were of serious concern to lumbermen and farmers alike.

In April 1882, the first American Forestry Congress was convened in Cincinnati, reconvening in Montréal in August of the same year. Ontario sent three delegates—a representative of the

---

Ontario's Provincial Foresters

Dr. Judson F. Clark was the first Provincial Forester, 1904–1906. A Canadian who was a professor of forestry at Cornell University he was appointed, in part, as a result of the 1899 Royal Commission's findings and Fernow's 1903 lectures at Queen's University. He was strongly opposed to the use of the Doyle Log Rule.

E.J. Zavitz was from southern Ontario and graduated in forestry from the University of Michigan. He taught forestry at the Ontario Agricultural College and briefly at the University of Toronto. He is regarded as the "father of reforestation" in Ontario, and his main focus was in the south. He was first appointed Provincial Forester in 1917 and held the post until 1926 when he became Deputy Minister of Forestry. In 1934 he was demoted from deputy and from then until 1941 resumed the title of Provincial Forester. The title disappeared until 1986 when K.A. Armson was appointed Provincial Forester and held that position until his retirement in 1989. He was a professor of forestry for 26 years at the University of Toronto specializing in silviculture and forest soils. He joined the Ministry in 1978 to negotiate with the forest industry what were to become the Forest Management Agreements (FMA's) under which the forest companies took full responsibility for forest management.

Grafted White Pines

South of Highway 60 near
Madawaska and 30 kilometres
east of Algonquin Provincial
Park are two white pines
(one 25 metres in height,
the other 29 metres) joined
together by the fusion of two
branches 7.6 metres above
the ground. The distance
between the two trees at the
graft is 81 centimetres.

fruit growers industry, an entomologist and a professor of agriculture interested in reforestation. The prime concerns were the need to protect forests from fires, and the planting of trees for the protection of orchards and other crop lands.

In 1883, the Ontario government appointed R.W. Phipps as the newly established Clerk of Forestry. His first report[21] dealt comprehensively with the issues and the importance of forests. Phipps, and more especially, Alexander Kirkwood, the Clerk of Crown Lands, wanted to establish forest reserves. In 1892 Kirkwood was appointed as chair of a Royal Commission on Forest Reservation and a National Park. Other members included Phipps, and James Dickson who had surveyed the area that would become Algonquin Park. The Commission recommended that a large tract be reserved. A year later (1893), Algonquin Park was established by legislation as *"a public park and forest reservation, fish and game preserve, health resort and pleasure ground for the benefit, advantage and enjoyment of the people of the Province."* Algonquin was also a major source of timber, and it has continued to be managed for timber to the present, in addition to providing the other benefits set out in the original legislation.

A dichotomy existed between the protection of northern forests and the reforestation of the highly visible waste lands in southern Ontario. E.J. Zavitz, from southern Ontario had completed a report on the extent of waste lands by 1909[22]. He estimated that in Norfolk, Lambton, Simcoe, Northumberland and Durham counties there were more than 109,000 hectares of waste land that could be treated by reforestation.

Ontario opened a provincial forest tree nursery at St. Williams in Norfolk County in 1908 for the provision of trees. In 1911, the province passed the Counties Reforestation Act which provided for municipalities to issue debentures up to $25,000 for the purchase of lands to be reforested. The municipalities did not see this as an incentive and there was virtually no response. Apart from improved fire protection services, there was little movement in reforestation during this time, although a number of ancillary developments were occurring which would stimulate major action in the field before too long.

Ontario recognized the need for forestry professionals, and Dr. B.E. Fernow was invited to give a series of lectures on forestry at Queen's University in 1903. In 1907, he became Dean of the first Canadian Faculty of Forestry at the University of Toronto. In 1900,

K. A. Armson

the Canadian Forestry Association was founded by a group of concerned senior government persons and lumbermen. A meeting of the Canadian Forestry Association in 1906, opened by the Governor General of Canada, Earl Grey, was addressed by the Prime Minister, Sir Wilfrid Laurier, R. L. Borden, and Gifford Pinchot from the United States. Pinchot noted that, *"...unless we can specify what forestry can do for us in Canada and the United States we may very well consider that we have failed in the presentation of our case... every school child, every boy and girl who passes from the primary into high school shall know what forestry means...."* The focus of the meeting was on the need to maintain the productivity of Canada's forests for timber, as well as for other values such as watershed protection. As A.P. Pross[23] put it, *"By 1900 forestry was fashionable... and in Canada the movement did not begin by being dominated by theorists or rabid conservationists."* Dr. Judson F. Clark, the recently appointed first Provincial Forester for Ontario attended the meeting, noting that while Canadian foresters could learn much from the foresters of Europe and the United States, *"... in the end they must work out their own salvation by development of a system of Canadian forest management designed especially to meet Canadian forest conditions."* (It is perhaps a sad commentary that it was not until 90 years later that the standards for a Canadian system were established by the CSA International[24].) Clark also advocated a systematic stock-taking, i.e. inventory of the timber resources and the necessity of having trained, practical foresters.

How to prevent large forest fires became a main concern, particularly when loss of life was involved. The Baudette-Rainy River fire in October, 1910 burned over 120,000 hectares, killing 42 people. A year later, in 1911 the Porcupine fire, which originated in areas where mining was prominent, swept through Timmins and decimated an area of approximately 200,000 hectares. At least 73 persons died, and the fire extended to the north and east as far as Cochrane. In 1916 the Matheson fire, killed 224 persons as it swept through an area of settlement, and forest, covering more than 340,000 hectares.

The Matheson fire galvanized the government into action; the Forests Fires Prevention Act was passed in 1917. It provided for the appointment of a Provincial Forester to administer the legislation, in addition to assuming responsibility for reforestation and tree diseases. E.J. Zavitz was appointed as Provincial Forester. His

Photo courtesy Algonquin Provincial Park

organization was called the Ontario Forestry Branch. The creation of a new bureaucratic organization did not mean that large fires were at an end. The Haileybury fire, began in October 1922 and burned over 200,000 hectares, destroying the towns of Charlton, Haileybury and North Cobalt as well as damaging New Liskeard and Englehart. 43 persons were killed and 6,000 lost their homes. Today, large forest fires still occur but without the devastating loss of life of earlier days.

The first World War (1914–1918) sent the forest industry into high gear, particularly the newly developing pulp and paper sector. Whereas the initial exploitation of eastern white and red pine flowed from the Napoleonic wars, Ontario's burgeoning logging of its northern forests reflected the stimulus of yet another European conflict. Thus, by 1919, there was a well-developed industry felling the spruce forests of the north, analogous to the way in which the pine forests of central Ontario had been logged in the previous century.

Two additional factors came into play: Ontario now had a small but growing body of professional foresters both in industry and government and the provincial election of 1919 saw the United Farmers of Ontario form the government with E.C.Drury as Premier. Drury, a graduate of the Ontario Agricultural College lived in Simcoe County where some of the most extensive pine forests had been logged. He had been a member of the forestry committee of the Ontario Agricultural and Experimental Union and was a friend of E.J. Zavitz. This professional forester—politician combination formed the real beginnings of reforestation in southern Ontario.

Drury's government also had concerns for the north, but these were largely overshadowed by ongoing scandals relating to timber licensing due, in part, to lax supervision of regulations.

Newton Apple

A lone apple tree of modest proportions stands on the grounds of the National Research Council in Ottawa. It is said to be a direct descendant of the famous tree under which Sir Isaac Newton lay when struck by a falling apple which led to his theory of gravity. The variety is uncertain.

K. A. Armson

Last Raft of Square Timber Floated Down The Ottawa River

The photograph from which this picture is made was taken in 1901, from Queen's Wharf, Ottawa. It shows Nepean Point, a rocky promontory overlooking the river, and one of the piers of the Interprovincial Bridge, then in course of erection, finished in 1903. The raft is nearly completed. It was the last to float down the Ottawa River, over the slides at Ottawa and thence down the St. Lawrence to Quebec. The raftsmen slept in the small house, and the large caboose was used for cooking. Near at hand is seen the tug in readiness to tow the timber to Quebec for shipment to England.

Photo courtesy Metropolitan Toronto Library Board.

1921 to 1950 *F*orestry Begins Then Stalls

On April 12, 1920, the Timber Commission, which consisted of Justices W.R. Riddell and F.R. Latchford—the latter an amateur zoologist, was appointed to investigate reported irregularities and possible illegal activities apparently rife in the timber operations on Crown lands. The Commission held hearings in Toronto, Sudbury, Port Arthur and Fort Frances and wasted no time, submitting three interim reports in July, October and November the same year, with its final report delivered in 1922.

What they found was incredible—an almost total lack of government control over the volume of wood cut. The licensee reported what was harvested and documents were not kept up-to-date. The justices concluded, *"The system followed by the Department would not be tolerated in any business institution.".* ... *"The Province must realize that loose methods in respect of our timber resources should not be permitted to continue."* The Commission also recommended that a more accurate rule than the Doyle Rule be used, (as Dr. Judson Clark had noted more than a decade before) yet Doyle would remain the official log rule in Ontario for another 30 years, until 1952.

The Commissioners identified a major obstacle to practising forestry, *"It does not appear that there is an adequate knowledge of the extent and character of the timber resources of the province and Crown lands generally"*, again echoing a concern of Judson Clark.

Reforestation was an important consideration. One of the key witnesses to the Commission on this subject was a company forester, Ben F. Avery, who as Chief Forester for the Spanish River Pulp and Paper Company had initiated a company forestry program aimed at providing a sustained timber supply. The Justices noted, *"Next to the necessity of preserving our existing Timber resources comes that of reinstating, so far as is practicable, what has been or will be utilized or destroyed.*" Based on information provided by Avery they concluded that, "*A company should have a reserve 40 times greater than that needed for one year's supply; but if a pulp company has such areas reserved for it, it would be proper to require it to cut so as to leave the whole territory in as good or almost as good a position as at first, thus assuring a perpetual supply.*"

Also of concern to the Commissioners was the scenic value of the forest landscape. In a section on the "*Destruction of Natural Beauty,*" they noted, "*...immediate utilization of the timber areas should not be permitted to destroy this beauty altogether more than is absolutely necessary.... Beauty is more and more an asset as civilization advances and settlement is increased; and a thing of beauty should be not only a joy but also a source of revenue forever.*" Surely a remark that presaged the maxim of "sustainable development" of the past two decades!

As often happens, organizations act upon anticipated recommendations of commissions before they are formally reported. In 1920, the Department of Lands and Forests undertook a forest survey of 8,640,000 acres (3,496,560 hectares) in northeastern Ontario[25]. The survey covered the north portion of what was the pulpwood licence to the Abitibi Power and Paper Company of Iroquois Falls, and the east side of what became the licence area for Spruce Falls Power and Paper Company. It was designed to provide a documentation of timber for those areas prior to logging.

Although the province had conducted exploratory surveys previously (as for example in 1900 when the Department of Crown Lands explored an area of some 60 million acres or 24.3 million hectares north of the Canadian Pacific Railway), the James Bay survey was important in several respects. It was planned and supervised by trained professional foresters, and it utilized aerial sketch mapping by observers to provide the base map information to survey staff for sampling on the ground.

The area was separated into the James Bay coastal plain in the north consisting of 5.83 million acres (2.35 million hectares) of which 93 per cent, consisting of muskeg, dwarf spruce, burn and water, was non-timbered. The lower, southern portion of the area, termed the Northern Clay Belt, occupied 2.80 million acres (1.13 million hectares), of which 39 per cent was timbered and 61 per cent was non-timbered. Twenty-two per cent of the entire area was classed as "burn," with proportions slightly higher in the clay belt

American Chestnut

(Castanea dentata)

Sault Ste. Marie, is home to

a native American Chestnut

with a diameter at breast

height (1.4 metres above

the ground) of 40 centimetres

and height of 15.5 metres.

timbered area than in the coastal one. Black spruce was the dominant species occupying 64 per cent of the total area, and 22 per cent of the timbered area of the northern clay belt.

The Ontario Forestry Branch also conducted annual forest surveys in other parts of the province, and in 1931[26], published the first comprehensive report of the province's forests, excluding southern Ontario. The total area covered was 73 million acres (29.5 million hectares); 48 million acres (19.4 million hectares) were surveyed by the Branch; data for 7 million acres (2.83 million hectares) came from inventories conducted by pulp and paper companies, and a further set of information on 13 million acres (5.26 million hectares) for the Kenora-Patricia area in northwestern Ontario came from Dominion of Canada topographical surveys. The Forestry Branch surveys used aerial sketching as standard procedure, although it was recognized that aerial photography would soon become the accepted procedure. In 1929 the Department purchased a Vedette aircraft specifically for this purpose. A map of the eight forest regions is shown in Figure 5-26.

Table 5-3. Comparisons of Age Class distribution by Per Cent for Conifer Types, 1930 and 1996. N.B. 1996 data for 20-year age classes grouped to match the broader divisions of the 1930 data. 1996 data also includes southern Ontario

Age Class	Young	Second Growth	Mature
1930	16	15	69
1996	18	37	44

K. A. Armson

PROVINCE OF ONTARIO

FORESTRY BRANCH

DEPARTMENT OF LANDS AND FORESTS

HON. W. FINLAYSON, MINISTER

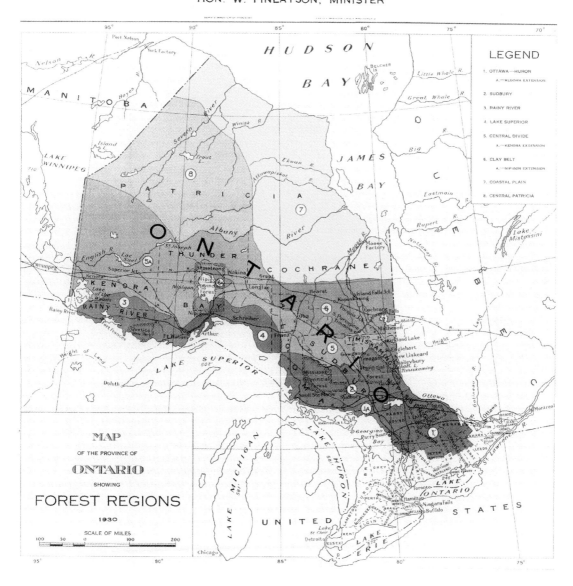

Figure 5-26.

Map of eight forest regions of Ontario, as of the 1930 forest inventory.

From Sharpe, J.F. and J.A. Brodie, 1931. The Forest Resources of Ontario.

Montgomery Oak

Straddling a front lawn on Old Oak Road is a large bur oak with a diameter at d.b.h. of 147 centimetres, a height of 23.5 metres and a crown spread of 26 metres. This specimen is located near the famed Montgomery Inn, a beautiful fieldstone structure erected in the 1830s by Thomas Montgomery, one of Etobicoke's early Irish settlers.

Ontario's forests were classified into three main types: conifer, hardwood, and mixedwood. The first two required a minimum 80 per cent of the trees specified in its class, while mixedwoods made up the balance. Forests were further identified as to age class—mature, second growth, young growth—and whether they were located in a recent burn area or barren and muskeg. Although the forests varied between the eight regions, the mature age class was largest in coniferous forests. The hardwood type was of significance only in the Ottawa-Huron region—corresponding to the central portion of the present Great Lakes – St. Lawrence region. The mixedwood type ranged from a low of 16 per cent of the forest area in the Rainy River region to a high of 52 per cent in the Central Divide region. In the Rainy River and Clay Belt regions, recent burns constituted 29 and 24 per cent, respectively, of the total forest area.

Overall, the mixedwood type was the largest at 39 per cent, while the unbalanced age class, with more than two-thirds mature in the coniferous type, was significant. Table 5-3 shows a comparison of the conifer age classes from the 1996 forest inventory approximated to the classes used in the 1930 survey. This suggests that over the six or so decades the imbalance has moderated with a significant decrease in the mature age class, a corresponding increase in "second growth," and little change in the young age class.

In addition to undertaking the provincial forest inventory, protection from forest fires continued to remain a major occupation. Bush telephone systems were built for better communication, fire towers were constructed to aid in identifying and locating fires, and the fire ranger system was generally overhauled, as the province attended to the provision of fire fighting equipment, and improved transportation services. The newly-formed provincial air service (1924) would become a major factor in Ontario's forest fire fighting program. The reason for the rapid acceptance of aircraft was twofold. First, there were the recent memories of the disastrous Haileybury forest fire of 1922 and the subsequent loss of life. Second, use of aircraft as a forest survey tool, and in identifying fires, had already been established by a forester, Reg. N. Johnston[27], who had been a pilot in the Royal Flying Corps in World War I.

The Forestry Branch also instituted a program of reforestation in southern Ontario, particularly on the Agreement Forests. The first Agreement Forest, the Hendrie Tract of Simcoe County Forest,

K. A. Armson

was located not far from Premier Drury's farm. Locations of larger areas of "wastelands," mainly sandy soils which had been 'farmed out' and eroded, had been identified by Zavitz in 1908, and it was in these areas that major reforestation took place.

Figure 5-27
"Farmed out" sandy wastelands
Note old pine stumps

Photo courtesy Ontario Ministry
of Natural Resources

Initially, seedlings came from St. Williams Nursery in Norfolk County, later from two new nurseries established in 1922 at Midhurst in Simcoe County and Orono in Durham County. Just over a million seedlings were produced in 1922, but by 1930, annual production was over 8 million, and, with some variation, remained about 10 million until 1945. Red pine was the favoured species because it was the most successful in surviving and growing on the well-drained, impoverished sands. Jack pine was used in the areas of active erosion, the so-called "blow-holes," and eastern white pine grew well on the finer textured sands where there was greater supply of soil moisture. Red pine was largely without major insect or disease problems in the first decades of its use, but this changed as the stands grew into polewood size. Eastern white pine, when planted in the open, often suffered repeated attacks by the white pine weevil, but was less susceptible when planted in a mixture with another species such as red pine (the red pine would shade the white, providing less favourable conditions for the female weevil to lay eggs on the eastern white pine shoots).

David Gibson Apples

Two 'Tolman Sweet' apple trees are remnants of an orchard planted by David Gibson in 1832 at what is now the corner of Yonge Street and Park Home Avenue in North York. David Gibson was a Reform member of the Legislative Assembly of Upper Canada and one of William Lyon Mackenzie's chiefs during the 1837 Rebellion. He was put in charge of government prisoners at Montgomery's Inn.

The long term effect of the Agreement Forests, and subsequently other private land forestry programs, was to increase significantly the amount of productive forest in southern Ontario from what it had been in the late 1800s.

The importance of farm woodlots in Ontario was also recognized although there was no special program dealing with them during the 1920s and 1930s. These woodlots continued to be used as a source of fuelwood, timber and, in many instances, for grazing—this latter use the most destructive since not only was the vegetation, including hardwood regeneration, consumed, but the soil was invariably compacted. In times of economic stress the farm woodlot was often treated as a cash asset, and clearcut. While this was not desirable, many of these woodlots when left to regenerate naturally, over time, became highly productive of quality species and timber.

The federal Commission on Conservation, also undertook surveys of natural resources, including forests and forest regeneration. Their Trent Watershed survey in 1912, was the first organized forest survey in the province. Formed in 1909[28], the Commission was active until 1920 when it was disbanded. One of the last forest surveys it completed was of the Goulais River watershed north of Sault Ste. Marie. This forest area was part of the pulpwood supply for the Spanish River Pulp and Paper company's mill in Sault Ste. Marie. Ben F. Avery, its Chief Forester, with the support of his company, undertook one of the first attempts to place a commercial forest operation on a sustained yield basis. The woods where spruce had been logged had substantial accumulations of dry slash which provided ample fuel for forest fires, which in turn resulted in the loss of any remaining small advanced spruce. White spruce, which was common on the better drained soils, was not adapted to regenerate after fire, and consequently the forest reverted mainly to poplars and white birch with more balsam fir than in the unlogged stands. Avery recognized that more effective and rapid detection of fires was essential if any investment was to be made in silvicultural practices. He initiated improved cutting practices, and established a nursery to produce spruce seedlings for planting in cutovers. He also saw that the rapid turnover of woodsworkers, and the seasonal nature of their employment, were major handicaps to ensuring the integration of logging and regeneration activities.

The second company to embark on a reforestation program

was the Abitibi Power and Paper Company at Iroquois Falls[29]. H.G.Schanche was the Manager of Abitibi's Forest Department, and although his first attempt at developing a nursery near the Twin Falls power dam in 1920 was a failure, his second, located on well-drained sands, fared much better. Of the 4.3 million seedlings produced by the Abitibi nurseries, only a small fraction, about ten per cent, were of a quality and suitable size to be planted out in the forest. In 1948, a survey of the outplanted trees revealed that of the nearly half million that had been planted, only about 61,000 could be considered in satisfactory condition after just over 20 years' growth. The lesson learned was: if investments are to be made in regenerating forests, then healthy planting stock, protection from fire, insects and disease, and proper maintenance to ensure the desired species are not overgrown by competing vegetation must be paramount requirements. In 1924, Schanche's staff developed a model to explore the options for investment in silviculture; a model that was virtually identical to those today, except that we now have better information and data on anticipated growth and yields from regenerated forests in the north over the past 30 to 40 years.

Figure 5-28
The Benner woodlot in southwestern Ontario. Clearcut for fuelwood 1918, viewed 53 years later.

In 1927, under a new Forestry Act, the province established a Forestry Board for, *"the purpose of studying all questions dealing with the problems of making the forest industries of this province permanent by the securing of continuous forest crops."* The members of the Board were E.J. Zavitz (Ontario Forestry Branch), B.F. Avery (Spanish River Pulp and Paper Co.), H.G. Schanche (Abitibi Power and Paper Co.), J.A. Gillies (Gillies Lumber Co.), and Dr. C.D. Howe (Faculty of Forestry, University of Toronto). As a result of the Board, a research section under the direction of J.A. Brodie was established and staffed in 1929. The Board was probably also influential in bringing about the Pulpwood Conservation Act of 1929—which required pulp companies provide to the government, forest inventories of their limits, and to plan their woodlands' activities on a sustained yield basis.

Unfortunately, the stock market crash of 1929, the ensuing depression in the 1930s, and the government of Mitchell Hepburn elected in 1934, meant that forestry programs of both industry and government came to a standstill until the end of World War II.

Exploitative logging of the forests continued, however, and production of eastern white and red pines in the Great Lakes–St. Lawrence Region was much reduced. Natural regeneration was minimal[30], usually occurring only on the drier well-drained areas of outwash sands. White pine regeneration required a suitable seedbed, usually the result of a fire, and a seed source. Where the pines were logged in mixed-wood stands (and a large proportion of this type were), the forest reverted mainly to broad-leaved species. We noted earlier that the removal of the desired spruce species from the mixedwood forests of the north would cause a transition in the forest to poplar, white birch and balsam fir.

When extensive areas of black spruce were logged, especially on poorly-drained mineral soils or peats, the species would retain its dominancy, although it might pass through a period of more than a decade under alders growing on the shallower peats where there was some drainage.

Hosie (1953) reviewed 58 regeneration studies conducted by governments and companies from 1918 to 1951. He was concerned about using a uniform and scientifically sound methodology for assessing regeneration, because the different procedures used over

Figure 5-29

Area similar in location to that in Figure 5-30 showing strip clearcutting.

Photo courtesy, Kent Virgo

K. A. Armson

the years made valid comparisons difficult. Finally, however, he concluded: *"there appears to be a considerable area of our cut-over forest land, particularly the better quality sites, that are (sic) not reproducing satisfactorily either as to species or as to quantity."*

The manner in which the forest is logged, whether for sawlogs or pulpwood, is an important factor in determining what the next stand will be.

Logging, over the period of Hosie's study, was still a seasonal occupation, which meant that there was little to no activity in the woods during the frost-free period of the year. Felling was done manually, usually when the ground was frozen, with some snow cover protecting small conifer seedlings. Hauling the wood to rivers or lakes on snow or ice roads meant little to no negative impact on the forest in terms of erosion.

The nature of the labour force was also a factor. Although attempts to unionize woodsworkers in Ontario date back to the early 1900s, the labour force remained fragmented, in part because of the seasonal nature of the work, but also because of the scattered and remote locations in which the labourers worked. Bush workers might be predominantly of one ethnic background depending on the area and company. French Canadians were more likely to be found in the northeastern part of the province while Finns made up a high proportion of the woods' labour force in Thunder Bay. These differences made it difficult for union organizers, over and above any resistance from the industry itself.

The majority of pulpwood cut was on a piecework basis. This practice had several results. It maintained a competitive atmosphere within the workforce, but also had an effect on the forest. Selection of the largest and best trees made for higher productivity to the cutter, and ignored the smaller yet still utilizable stems—an incentive to "highgrade" the forest. Company supervision was usually minimal, with the result that the most productive stands were harvested with minimal administrative costs. The larger pulp and paper companies usually assigned cutters to strips (Figure 5-29). Forests developing on areas cut in this manner retain these

Figure 5-30
Aerial view of black spruce "new" forest, 30 years after strip clearcutting in early 1950s

patterns to this day (Figure 5-30). Radforth (1987) has noted that, when workers were paid on a piecework basis, they insisted on using the tools with which they were familiar—the Swede saw (invented by a Finn) and the axe.

Wood was skidded out with horses, and any mechanization was essentially limited to truck hauls on roads of ice and snow. Railways were built to move logs to the mills—Abitibi Power and Paper Company at Iroquois Falls, Spruce Falls Power and Paper Company at Kapuskasing, and the Fasset Lumber Corporation in Algonquin Park.

A uniquely Canadian invention, the 'alligator'[31] or steam warping tug was used to move logs in the rivers and lakes. The alligator was first produced in 1889 by West and Peachey at their factory in Simcoe, Norfolk County, Ontario, as a result of a request by local developer, John Jackson, who had acquired timber limits inland from Georgian Bay on a tract which was only accessible via the French and Restoule rivers. Prior to the alligator's appearance, logs were moved in the lakes by warping. A capstan was mounted on a cadge crib; several hundred feet of large manilla rope attached to a warping anchor was wound around the capstan. The process was laborious; the capstan was turned either manually or with horses. Supplies and equipment required portaging. Jackson knew that West and Peachey had built steam engines, and even a small steam powered boat. He wanted something that would enable him

Figure 5-31
Alligator steam warping tug, owned by Dickson Lumber Co., Peterborough.

Photo courtesy Clarence F. Coons

K. A. Armson

to get his logs through the combination of lakes and streams more efficiently. More than 200 alligators were produced between 1889–1934, and used by forest companies, primarily in Ontario and Québec, but also in the United States and South America.

The mid 1930s brought considerable labour unrest and strikes to the industry. Conditions in the bush camps, which had been primitive at best, gradually improved but, except for the use of machines in hauling wood, mechanization of logging would not begin significantly until after World War II.

The financial instability of several pulp and paper companies, coupled with political and public concerns about the administration of Crown forests, led to the appointment of a Selective Committee of the Legislature in 1939, to examine the manner in which the Department of Lands and Forests handled the province's natural resources. Neither the report of the Committee, nor a minority report submitted by George Drew, leader of the opposition Conservative Party, served to satisfy public concerns. The fact that Canada was at war, also meant that there would be no direct changes to the administration of Ontario's forests.

What did occur was a total reorganization of the Department of Lands and Forests in 1941, with the appointment of Frank A. MacDougall as Deputy Minister. MacDougall was a forester who had served in World War I and graduated in forestry in 1923 from the University of Toronto. He had joined the Department, serving in Pembroke and Sault Ste. Marie where he was responsible for the reforesting of agricultural wastelands and the establishment of the Kirkwood Forest near Thessalon. Prior to his appointment as Deputy Minister, he had been the Superintendent of Algonquin Park. Not only was MacDougall an excellent administrator with an ability to anticipate opportunities that might arise in the political arena, he also recognized a clear distinction between Minister and the Deputy Minister as to who was in charge of the day-to-day running of the Department. MacDougall brought a high degree of professionalism to his work, coupled with an understanding of the importance of integrating timber, wildlife and other uses—in other words, the concept of integrated management and multiple use. He knew the importance of establishing a sense of collegiality within his staff, while also allowing them to take responsibility and act on their own initiatives.

With the end of the war in 1945, public and political concerns about forestry, which had lain dormant since 1940, emerged. The

Comfort Maple

A giant maple in North Pelham (Niagara County) is 25 metres high and 75.1 centimetres in diameter. This tree is on property which was formerly owned by James and Laura Secord (1814–16) and the Comfort family.

Conservative government, which had been elected under George Drew, appointed a Royal Commission on Forestry in 1946. Major General Howard Kennedy was its Commissioner. The terms of the Commission and the Commissioner's report[32] covered the forestry gamut, including private woodlands. In reviewing the history of Ontario's forests, Kennedy noted, *"It is apparent that public apathy, selfish interests of individuals and sometimes political expediency have, in the past, all had a share in delaying the rational utilization of our forests."* He readily appreciated the dynamic nature of the resources: *"Another striking impression is that of the tremendous capacity of the forests to heal the wounds made by both man and nature. It is amazing how the appearance of once devastated areas changes in a quarter of a century."*

The report made many recommendations, but its main focus was on the need to improve the utilization of the Crown's timber and to eliminate waste; *"I am convinced that senior executives, who demand the highest standards in housekeeping and prevention of waste in their mills, would be horrified if they were to travel over their cut-over areas and see the waste of material and effort in the woods."* The problem then, as now, was that executives do not go to the woods unless on a "sanitized" tour; wood has always been available and the woodlands are a cost not a profit centre. Woodlands' managers know this well, since they are often burdened with costs placed on them by their superiors that have nothing directly to do with wood production.

A choice example comes from the Québec and Ontario Paper Company owned by the *Chicago Tribune* newspaper. The company built a paper mill at Thorold in 1913 and then, in the mid to late 1930s, another mill at Baie-Comeau on Québec's north shore in a very isolated location. A company town had to be built for the workers, and they and their families provided for. Chairman, Colonel Robert McCormick, described the efforts of his firm as follows: *"Milk was not used on the North Shore, but we were*

Felling pine trees 1919.
Austin Nicholson Lumber Co.
22 miles west of Chapleau off
main CPR Line.

Photo courtesy
Ontario Dept. of Lands and Forests

K. A. Armson

remaking the North Shore. Milk had to be provided. This could be provided only by cows living exclusively on hay and oats; there was no pasture land there. It was pointed out that the cost of such milk was beyond the means of the workers. This impasse was overcome by charging the normal price for milk and charging the difference to the cost of pulpwood."[33]

The most sweeping recommendation of the Kennedy Commission—a plea for a completely new concept in the allocation and operation of Crown lands, and the establishment of Forest Operating companies based on major watersheds—was ignored. The Commission envisioned these companies as harvesting and regenerating partnerships between individuals and mills obtaining timber from the area. Interestingly, this thinking anticipated the development of such partnerships on former Crown management units, following their transformation to Sustainable Forest Licences in the late 1990s, although locations were not chosen on a watershed basis.

Some of the Commissioner's concerns for making more support available to woodlot owners and conservation authorities of southern Ontario were already recognized by provincial administrators and were gradually being addressed. The property destruction and loss of life precipitated by hurricane "Hazel" in November 1954, however, moved the Conservation Authority issue into full crisis mode. A report which had been tabled by a committee of the legislature[34] in 1950, making recommendations for flood control and the establishment of conservation authorities in southern Ontario, was now acted upon. Ontario's conservation authorities were reorganized. A combination of provincial and municipal financial funds provided significant improvements to their development and operations, particularly in education and in the recreational use of their lands.

The Kennedy Commission's recommendations on timber management within the Department were essentially about

Felling White pine
Flame Lake Camp,
Chapleau (1948)

Photo courtesy
Ontario Dept. of Lands and Forests

Treaty Oak

It was under the branches of this red oak on King Street, Niagara-on-the-Lake that treaty money was paid to Indians by the first Indian agent in Canada. The tree had a girth of 647.7 centimetres. Only a remnant remains today.

increasing administrative efficiencies. In 1946, the Department assumed responsibility for Game and Fisheries management. This was further expanded in 1954 when it took over responsibility for parks, in keeping with the Commission's philosophy of developing a cohesive policy of Natural Resource management.

Insect destruction to agricultural crops and forests has long been a problem in Ontario. Artist Paul Kane travelling through the Lake of the Woods in 1846, noted 150 miles (240 km.) of forest stripped by forest tent caterpillars (*Malacosma disstria* Hbn.); this was the same pest that damaged fruit trees in southern Ontario during the mid to late 1800s. The Kennedy Commission recognized the need for insect control, and was very much aware of the devastating outbreak of spruce budworm that had occurred in northern and central Ontario in the early 1940s, including an outbreak in Algonquin Park. Jack pine budworm was also prevalent through the late 1930s, but because spruce was the major pulpwood species, it was the spruce budworm which drew public attention. These outbreaks were disturbing to the industry, and in 1943, the Minister of Lands and Forests convened a meeting[35] of provincial, and federal (Department of Agriculture, Ottawa) officials, and industry representatives, to consider the spruce budworm issue. Four main recommendations flowed from this meeting. All were acted upon.

1. The undertaking of a large-scale aerial application experiment to control the insect. In fact, aerial application of calcium arsenate to control hemlock looper (*Lambdina fiscellaria fiscellaria* (Guen.)) in the Muskoka Lakes area, at Lake Joseph and Ahmic Lakes, and spruce budworm at Westree (Gogama district), had been done in 1928, and again at Westree in 1929. 1,700 acres (688 hectares) of forest at Ahmic and Lake Joseph, were treated with calcium arsenate at a rate of 28 kg per hectare. In June 1944, the Department aerially applied DDT using 100 lbs. (45.4 kg) per infested area in Algonquin Park.

2. Provision for specific facilities at the University of Toronto for special forestry training at undergraduate and graduate levels. In 1945, a chair in forest entomology was established, initially financed by the Ontario forest industry. Dr. Carl E. Atwood, previously in charge of federal forest insect investigations in the province, was appointed to the position in 1946.

K. A. Armson

3. The building of a central laboratory for research into forest insect problems. By agreement between the federal Department of Agriculture and the Department of Lands and Forests, a structure was already planned for Sault Ste. Marie. It was completed in 1946, paid for by the province, but staffed by the federal Department of Agriculture.

4. The development of a more effective system for the detection of insects. The Department of Lands and Forests employed seven forest insect rangers, ultimately transferring them to the federal staff.

Ontario also asked the federal government to increase its budget for forest insect work in the province by $200,000. Turner (1965) does not record an action on this request.

In 1948, Ontario's forests suffered from a series of fires, one of the largest of which occurred in the central part of the province around Chapleau when two separate conflagrations joined to create what is now known as the Mississagi Fire. Mississagi covered more than 260,000 hectares and destroyed a large area of commercially mature timber, including much jack pine.

Historically sawmills in the Chapleau and Blind River region had been set up to utilize large eastern white pine; they were basically unsuitable for the smaller jack pine. Standing timber after a burn is very susceptible to beetles which can quickly destroy its value. The Ontario government wanted to salvage the burned timber as rapidly as possible and a number of small sawmillers from Québec set up their mills in the region. The Dubreuils, Malettes, Martels, and Lafrenières answered the call and remained in the area to establish a new generation of mills—following, rather than preceding the earlier pulp and paper mill establishment. These operations became competitors for sawlog-size spruce and pine already licensed to the larger pulp and paper companies; this competition created a continuing source of controversy for years to come. It was not until the early 1960s, when technology in the form of chip-n-saw would bring about a nexus between these two groups. Pulp mills found a readily usable and cheap supply of chips from the sawmills, while sawmills, in turn, found a merchantable product for what used to be wasted or burned as slabs and edgings.

White Ash

(Fraxinus americana)

Located on King St.

Niagara-on-the-Lake,

this tree has a diameter of

127 centimetres with

a height of 31.4 metres.

Although Ontario's forests and the management of provincial Crown lands are a provincial responsibility, cooperation between the two levels of government makes sense in areas where expertise and facilities may lie in one jurisdiction or be split between the two. Such cooperation often involves the forest industry, as industry has much to lose or gain from government decisions and actions respecting the timber supply. In 1949, a significant piece of legislation, the Canada Forestry Act (1949), was passed, which allowed a federal Minister to enter into agreements with any province, *"for the protection, development or utilization of forest resources, including protection from fire, insects and diseases, forest inventories, silvicultural research, watershed protection, reforestation, forestry publicity and education, construction of forest roads and improvements of streams in forest areas, improvement of growing conditions and management of forests for continuous production."* This was to be the basis for a remarkable impetus to forestry, not only in Ontario, but throughout Canada.

Winter sleigh haul, 1950.

K. A. Armson

1951 to 1980 *F*orestry Regenerated

A first requirement, if intelligent decisions are to be made about forestry objectives and activities, is to have a relatively up-to-date, quantifiable assessment of the forest estate. This was recognized by the head of the Division of Timber Management[36], Ontario Department of Lands and Forests, who stated, *"Perhaps one of the greatest handicaps to our progress in forestry has been the lack of a proper inventory of the forest resources."* The forest inventory of 1930 was an initial step towards this goal, but 20 years later, a new inventory was long overdue, and its accomplishment became a main task for the Timber Management Division of the Department of Lands and Forests. To meet this challenge, the Forest Resources Inventory (FRI) section employed large numbers of newly-graduated foresters—many veterans from the armed forces of World War II—who spent their summers doing the field work in the forests, compiling their data during the winters in Toronto. When the inventory was completed, most of these foresters were posted as timber management foresters to the Department's districts. Despite their title, however, they were primarily concerned with timber allocation, wood measurement (scaling) and the administration of licences to industry. Funding of the forest provincial inventory and northern reforestation in the 1950s flowed from a 1952 federal-provincial forestry agreement, which included forest fire protection in 1957–58. This agreement was the forerunner of several Federal-Provincial Forest Resource Development Agreements (FRDA's) which would continue until the 1990s.

The major use of funds for reforestation on Crown lands in Ontario's north went to the development of nurseries. In 1952, there were only three: a provincial nursery at Fort William (Thunder Bay) which had been established on the initiative of the

Regional Forester, Peter Addison in 1946; one at Moonbeam near Kapuskasing, established in 1947 by the Spruce Falls Power and Paper Company to provide seedlings primarily for the company's freehold forest land; and a third established in 1951 at Longlac by Kimberly-Clark. By the early 1960s the Department had established new nurseries at Dryden, White River, Chapleau, Swastika, Gogama, and Thessalon.

Figure 5-32

Boulders used for site preparation, Beardmore 1962

Photo, courtesy Fred C. Robinson

In 1952, a "new" Crown Timber Act reflected a more organized approach to forest management. Forest companies were still responsible for planning, and for the regeneration of the Crown forest lands on which they harvested. Crown forests were divided into 123 forest management units (including 36 company units which were essentially the existing forest company timber licence areas). The remaining 87 units were designated as Crown units, many of which located in areas where short-term licencees and sawmills had cutting rights. A few years earlier three units[37], the Kirkwood Forest Management Unit (1943) near Thessalon, Petawawa Management Unit (1945) consisting of predominantly eastern white and red pine forests in the northeastern portion of Algonquin Park, and the Englehart Management Unit (1945) in boreal jack pine and spruce, had been formally established. The Petawawa Unit attracted the most attention and effort.

The 1950s marked the beginning of forest management planning at the unit level, using a provincially established methodology. It did not mean that the forests were now being managed. Rather, allocations of areas for logging were being scrutinized and monitored more carefully.

The Petawawa Unit began a series of attempts at modifying the harvesting method to produce natural regeneration of eastern white and red pines using a silvicultural shelterwood system. In the 1950s, Abitibi Paper Company at Raith (northwest of Thunder Bay) embarked on an ambitious program of experimental harvesting patterns to regenerate spruce and jack pine. Spruce Falls Power and Paper Company began handplanting in the openings of cut strips, and the Englehart Crown Unit initiated a plan to use a silvicultural clearcutting system followed by planting.

Earliest plantings by Department staff were mainly on small open areas in Crown Units, often those which had been burned after clearcutting. From the start there were problems in attempting

K. A. Armson

to change harvesting patterns. Neither the companies nor bush-workers involved wanted to modify their usual procedures because to do so would result in higher company costs, lower wages to the cutter and lower productivity overall. Tree planting was seasonal, and most northern forestry staff considered it an additional burden to their regular duties. Planting stock was often of poor quality, and planters too often were drifters looking to earn a few quick dollars before moving on. If the seedlings did manage to survive for a few years, competing vegetation usually guaranteed minimal growth and low survival over the longer term.

The Department transferred some reforestation foresters from southern Ontario to the northern districts, but procedures and stock used in the south did not work well. It was clear that if cutover lands, usually with heavy slash accumulation and much competing vegetation, were to be regenerated by planting, some form of site preparation was necessary. Recognizing this, the Timber Management Division organized "Project Regeneration" in 1956, and toured the north with heavy equipment, some of which had been used successfully in the southeastern United States to prepare recent cutovers for planting southern pines. Although Project Regeneration was organized by the Timber Division, and not the Reforestation Division, one year later in 1957, the two divisions were amalgamated, and in 1959 the new division received a new name, the Timber Branch.

Figure 5-33
Tractor pads and and chains used to scarify in jack pine cutovers.
Photo courtesy, Weyerhaeuser Canada, Dryden

Local staff experimented with local materials—boulders (Figure 5-32) or large poplar roots—in an attempt to create planting sites, but real success came with the development of barrels (Figure 5-37) around 1960. Another successful innovation was the use of a combination of tractor pads and chains to scarify jack pine cutovers (Figure 5-33). Heavy equipment use in site preparation of cutovers was possible because it was coincident with harvesting mechanization. The industry had known for a long time that productivity needed to be increased. This meant changing the way wood was cut, a process that required the involvement of the bush-workers.

Figure 5-34
Skidder with sawlog, 1965

The introduction of a lightweight, affordable chainsaw was a major breakthrough. In 1949–1950, less than one per cent of pulpwood cut in eastern Canada was cut with chainsaws; five years later, chainsaws accounted for more than 50 per cent of the cut. While this may seem an extremely rapid increase for such a short period, it should be remembered that the first chainsaw patent was issued in 1858, and the first chainsaw manufactured in the United States was in 1917. Ross Silversides remarked (1997): *"The development of the chainsaw represents one of the longest lead-in times in the history of mechanical technology."* Two necessary steps were the mechanization of the actual harvesting and the movement of wood piles to more central areas for loading and transport to the mill.

As often happens, early machines were adaptations of already existing models used in agriculture or elsewhere. Innovations developed rapidly and very little time passed before a series of machines like skidders (Figure 5-34, used to facilitate wood movement, either as logs or tree lengths) and forwarders (to facilitate movement of wood packages to more central points) were being used in many operations. Felling of the trees was still done manually, albeit with

K. A. Armson

a chainsaw, and this bottleneck led to a number of additional attempts at mechanization. One of the most successful was the tree harvester, which used shears. This was conceived and developed in Ontario by staff of the Marathon Paper Company. Between 1960 and 1970, 40 Beloit tree harvesters (Figure 5-35) were produced; the tree harvester concept laid the groundwork for the less massive fellers and feller bunchers.

Several other factors contributed towards the greater mechanization of harvesting over the next 30 years. First, was the push by the industry to increase productivity. Second, and very importantly, woodsworkers in Ontario, and the unions representing them did not fight the move to mechanize their work. As Ian Radforth (1987) noted, *"Overwhelmingly, woodsworkers and their union spokesmen welcomed the new logging equipment, and many of the new methods,"* largely because their earnings increased and the opportunities to improve their skills operating such equipment enhanced future employment possibilities. Third, without the concurrent development and availability of reliable hydraulic systems, efficient machines would not have been so readily possible. Fourth, mechanization was predicated on year-round operations, which meant that all-weather road systems had to be in place.

A number of implications arose from these changes which would have a profound effect on the forests, and on forest conditions after the logging process. New machines were costly to develop and produce so there was a push, both by manufacturers and by companies, to utilize them in as wide a range of conditions as possible. This meant that the machine impact on the environment was often negative. Skidders used on wet ground produced rutting. Large accumulations of slash, depending on the type of machine, could make tree regeneration, whether natural or planted, difficult if not impossible. Other machines might strip the forest floor to its mineral soil, reduce fertility and increase the possibility for erosion losses. The size and weight of many machines ensured that advanced regeneration of commercial tree species such as spruce was often destroyed, while standing commercial species not used were damaged or knocked over. Depending on the type of harvesting equipment, some companies

Figure 5-35
Beloit tree harvester

found it only profitable to operate in high volume and quality stands, continuing the 'highgrading' process practiced by manual pieceworkers during previous decades. Conversely, other companies cut over much larger areas in order to justify their equipment investment. Often, little attention was given to the way in which secondary and tertiary roads—the bush roads used by the logging machines—were located, maintained, or 'put to bed' after use. The result was erosion, disruption of drainage, and difficult, if not impossible access for subsequent regeneration work. Logging machine development was often the result of interest and actions of a few local individuals or companies, serving a single purpose.

The most significant productivity gains were made by combining equipment to produce a logging 'system'. Full tree harvesting with roadside delimbers and slashers left no piles of slash on the forest floor but stacked it into large piles at roadside. The development of wide tires by the Forest Engineering Research Institute of Canada (FERIC) was done to increase productivity of skidder operations (Figure 5-36); these tires rapidly became one of the most effective ways to reduce rutting, particularly on moist soils in the frost-free season.

Figure 5-36
Skidder with high flotation (wide) tires

K. A. Armson

Mechanization of harvesting brought a series of developments which would affect the 'new' forest significantly:

1. A greater proportion—up to five per cent—of the productive forest could now be left in roads or landings on which regeneration of commercial tree species would be slow to become established.

2. Mature commercial broadleaved species not utilized, such as poplar and white birch, generally died as a result of exposure, while other conifers were subjected to exposure and windthrow. The net result was that harvested forests of predominantly spruce or jack pine, in mixtures with poplar and white birch (which were usually of fire origin), regenerated mainly to poplar and white birch, usually with a balsam fir component some 20 to 30 years[38] after logging.

3. When summer logging of jack pine on well-drained sandy soils was done so that the slash with cones was well-distributed, it could be expected that jack pine would regenerate. The degree of success depended on the amount of forest floor disturbance because jack pine seeds germinate best in mineral soil.

4. Generally, regeneration of black spruce stands on poorly-drained soils decreased after mechanical logging compared to the regeneration which occurred after manual strip cutting because machinery caused damage to advanced growth, as well as physical damage to the wet soils. This situation was largely remedied in the early 1980s with the introduction of wide tracks and wide, high flotation tires.

5. Shrub species such as mountain ('moose') maple and alders would flourish on logged upland and lowland forests until a new canopy formed above. It might take several decades for tree species to form such a canopy.

Figure 5-37
Sharkfin barrels used in site preparation

As the industry was rapidly mechanizing its logging operations, the Department of Lands and Forests began to seriously tackle the business of regeneration, particularly on the Crown Management Units where they had complete control over both the harvesting and regeneration. In 1962 the Crown Timber Act was amended so that the forest companies were relieved of the responsibility for regeneration on all Crown lands. This was now assumed by the Department for three main reasons. First, many companies were not fulfilling their responsibilities. Second, there was a body of professional and technical expertise developing within the Department that was "straining at the bit" to get on with the job of reforestation of cutovers. Third, senior Department staff recognized that the time was appropriate both professionally and politically to assume full responsibility. For the Crown lands under licence, companies could enter into regeneration agreements whereby they would undertake certain activities such as site preparation while the Department would provide seed or planting stock and plant the cutovers if required. In the north, foresters and technicians, by trial and error mostly, focused on site preparation before planting or seeding as the early attempts in the 1950s had showed that some form of preparation was necessary. Now the challenge was to find out what would do the job efficiently. As happened with logging mechanization, site preparation equipment such as sharkfin barrels (Figure 5-37) which had worked well in one set of conditions might be totally unsuitable in other locations due to differences in soils, drainage, and slash conditions. Equipment that could be easily modified and used with existing power units employed in logging was more likely to be acceptable than large single purpose machines. The machine operators were accustomed to using their power units in logging and road building in a 'bulldozing'

Figure 5-38
A Bracke cultivator. The tines create patches of exposed soil at regular intervals and not a continuous strip.

manner and had to be trained to use a more sensitive touch with site preparation equipment to achieve the correct effect. Elsewhere in Canada, the United States and Scandinavia, foresters were busy trying out new equipment not only for site preparation, but also for planting, which on most forest cutovers was done manually. Some of the imported equipment worked well but often, they were too light for the heavy slash and rough terrain of bedrock and boulders so common to Ontario's forests. In time, however, the more versatile pieces such as the Bracke cultivator (Figure 5-38)and the TTS disk trencher became almost standard equipment in much of the province.

Most of the regeneration work involved seeding or planting following site preparation. Although there was a limited amount of modification of logging methods in the boreal forest, usually involving some form of strip cutting. This modification was only successful in black spruce. In the Great Lakes – St. Lawrence forest the shelterwood system, either uniform or more usually in strips, was employed to regenerate eastern white pine while strip clearcutting was used to regenerate yellow birch. The modified harvesting of this nature was primarily on Crown Management Units. Seeding became one of the major ways to regenerate jack pine and its development was essentially an Ontario 'first'. Although seeding has been employed in forestry for a hundred or more years, the ability to broadcast small seed such as that of jack pine over large areas rapidly and uniformly required an appropriate device that could be used on an aircraft or ground machine. Such a seeder (Figure 5-39) was designed and built by Howard Brohm of the Department's Research Division. Once the area to be seeded had been properly site prepared, usually in the summer prior to seeding, the seeding would be done in March before the snow cover had gone. This timing had two advantages. As the snow finally melted the water would carry the small seeds into the surface pores of the exposed soil where it would germinate relatively quickly. When ground machines were used with the Brohm seeder mounted on the rear, the driver could ensure a uniform distribution as he could see his tracks in the snow, and because of the snow cover there was a relatively even surface on which the seeds would fall. By regulating the number of seeds per area, the density of the regenerated new stands could be roughly controlled. This control was not possible when pads and chains were dragged over jack pine slash in cutovers (which was another way of successfully regenerating that species on certain soils and conditions) because it depended on seeds coming

Figure 5-39
A Brohm seeder mounted on a snowmobile

Sycamore

(American Sycamore—

plantanus occidentalis)

Located near Sydenham River,

south of Alvinston,

this tree has a diameter of

263 centimetres with

a height of 29.9 metres.

from cones opening on or near the ground. Aerial seeding using helicopters and fixed wing aircraft became a standard means of regenerating large harvested areas, and after forest fires.The technique of prescribed burning as a site preparation tool was used in certain districts, although its successful application was highly weather dependent. Another use of prescribed fire to prepare seed beds for regeneration of yellow birch was developed by the Department's research staff in the Great Lakes – St. Lawrence region, but little used operationally.

The major efforts and costs were devoted to planting, and the earlier difficulties associated with using bare root planting stock were now magnified. Although the northern nurseries were coming into production by the early 1960s, the stock often had to be shipped a hundred or more miles to the planting sites and packed, handled and stored on site with care. For the most part, Department staff at both the nurseries and in the field were new to this type of operation. With bare root stock, the planting season is a short period in the spring and a second one for spruce in the late summer to early fall. Because of the size of the planting operations, the earlier problems using transient labour were minimized, partly because they were not available in the numbers required, but mainly because the rates of pay and the outside work became attractive to students coming out of schools, colleges and universities in the spring. In addition, local persons and native peoples became involved in tree planting and the character of the planting work force changed. This change became even more dramatic with the introduction of container planting stock on a large scale, beginning in 1966. The hectic nature of the planting season and the fact that many of the early plantings were deemed failures required a change in strategy. In 1965 the Department undertook a massive and novel venture in container stock production, based on the results of trials undertaken during the previous 10 years. It was decided to locate in each of the northern districts, sets of plastic greenhouses (Figure 5-40) in which seedlings would be grown in small 5/8 inch (1.6 cm) diameter plastic tubes for a few weeks until they were barely beyond the cotyledonous stage. They would then be shipped out for planting, using a dibble stick. The operations of the plastic houses, which were oil heated, were the responsibility of the local Department staff, many of whom were neither trained nor interested in growing seedlings. It was planned to produce 20 million container seedlings in 1966, but only 17

K. A. Armson

million were actually produced for outplanting. The same year the conventional nurseries produced 49 million bare root stock. Four years later (1970) container stock production was down to 6 million while bare root had increased to over 62 million trees. In 1973 only 2.9 million containers were produced while 68 million bare root came out of the nurseries. It would be several years before container stock production would again become significant in Ontario, although at two of the northern nurseries, Thunder Bay and Swastika, staff took on the task of experimenting with different types of containers, and even integrating containers into the bare root program. The reasons for the decline of the "Ontario" tube and its eventual replacement by other, larger containers are instructive. A sudden massive introduction of a new system, from head office without proper introduction and training to the field staff who have to implement it made for a poor start. Small seedlings such as the ones in the Ontario tube would only survive if there was suitable site preparation; there had been little time to prepare for the sudden outplanting of 17 million seedlings and as a result many of the plantings were unsuccessful. Of the conifers, jack pine was the most successful. Experience in extending the planting season

Figure 5-40
Plastic houses to grow Ontario tube seedlings, 1966

through the summer, and the relative ease of planting containers, as compared with bare root stock, were positive outcomes and resulted in a major change in the planting workforce with many women, often from local communities, becoming planters. The need for satisfactory site preparation became readily apparent. With better organization and the longer season, tree planting became an opportunity for contractors, often those who had been planters themselves, either in Ontario or in other provinces such as British Columbia, to undertake planting.

In 1964 the Minister of Lands and Forests established a Forestry Study Unit to examine the existing forest resources of the province, study the forest-based industries, but primarily, *"...to assure that the forest resources will be used to the best advantage of the people of the Province..."*. The Unit's report in 1967[39], (the Brodie Report) made 70 recommendations dealing with virtually all aspects of forestry on both Crown and private lands including: cooperatives of licensees, that the management of forest land be put on a business basis, the expansion of the silviculture program and intensification of regeneration and tending, improvement in utilization by integrating sawlog and pulp operations, recognizing the possible impacts of the recent technology of "chip-n-saw".

Interior of plastic house with small seedlings in Ontario tubes ready to be planted

Many of the recommendations of the Brodie Report presaged changes which were to occur during the next few years or were being begun—for example, the Woodlands Improvement Agreement (WIA) program.

Another technology dramatically changed the utilization of Ontario's forests. Until 1970 relatively small amounts of poplar, mainly trembling aspen, were being used by a few pulp mills, although high quality aspen and white and yellow birch were used as veneer. Yellow birch in the Great Lakes – St. Lawrence forests had, from the late 1930s into the 1970s, been one of the most heavily exploited broadleaved trees in that region largely for veneer. The ability to use poplar, and to a limited degree other species, in a 'waferboard' panel began to increase demand for aspen in an unprecedented manner beginning in the 1970s. This demand increased further with the introduction of the 'oriented strand board' technology in the 1980s. The major increase in poplar

K. A. Armson

utilization meant that, particularly in boreal forests, residual poplar trees were no longer as much of a problem in preparing the sites for conifer regeneration. However, where forest management was the responsibility of a major licensee more interested in conifers, and the poplar licensee's interest was in leaving the cutover for poplar regeneration, conflicts became inevitable. This illustrates the type of problem that has arisen increasingly with the use of a licensing system basically 150 years old.

From the 1950s on, increasing recreational travel in Crown forests resulted in the public expressing concerns about not only logging, but the fact that it was being allowed in certain of the provincial parks, Algonquin Park in particular. This came to a head in 1968 when the Ministry released a Provisional Master Plan for the Park. The public debates about the plan and particularly about the provision for logging were heated. In response the government established a task force to review submissions and shortly thereafter, an advisory committee with broad representation to make recommendations to the Minister. Shortly after their report, made in 1973, the government decided to create a Crown Agency to take responsibility for all forest management in the park and cancel all existing licences held by operators.

Photo courtesy Algonquin Provincial Park

The Algonquin Forestry Authority[40] (AFA) became incorporated by law in January 1975, and still reports to the Minister of Natural Resources to the present day. The Authority operates only within the recreation-utilization zone within the park, and its activities over the past 25 years have provided an excellent example of how professional forest management can be applied in such visible and high use recreation areas for the benefit of all.

Until the late 1960s the planning and implementation of most timber management activities, particularly regeneration, was done on an annual basis. With the increasing size of the program and the fact that it was done on a piecemeal basis, district by district, senior forest resource staff realized the need for an overall policy or strategy so that objectives could be set for a provincial future wood supply. The strategy would also quantify the land base needed for timber production and provide a basis for a commitment to continuity of funding by government. In 1972, five options

Trembling Aspen

(Populus tremuloides)

Located in Limerick Township,

Hastings County; this tree has

a diameter of 80 centimetres

with a height of 38 metres.

were developed for size of land base, regeneration activities and costs to provide for a future timber supply in the year 2020. The Ontario Cabinet approved the option that would have in place an annual volume of 9.1 million cunits (25.8 million m3) of wood for industrial use. This was known as the Forest Production Policy[41]. Of the several assumptions that were made, one was that the "old", desirable, and accessible forest would be depleted by 2020, and the 25.8 million m3 would come from forests established since 1973. By the late 1980s it was obvious that this assumption was too pessimistic and significant supplies were still to come from the "old" forest, given the same land base. Within two years of the implementation of the Forest Production Policy, funding commitments by government had faltered and were no longer at the levels originally planned.

As the Ministry's work in reforestation became more extensive and sophisticated, and as silvicultural knowledge and expertise were obtained, it became apparent that the separation of the planning and carrying out of harvesting operations by the forest companies was often creating obstacles in the regeneration of cutovers by Ministry staff. Road access that should have been planned to be effective for both harvesting and reforestation was not occurring. Records and monitoring of the Ministry's work were too often inadequate or missing. Field forestry staff, especially foresters, were often less than five years in an area before moving to another one; thus continuity in observation and interest in longer-term results of reforestation were minimal. In 1975 the Ministry commissioned a study of forest management[42] and one of the major recommendations from it was that the Ministry consider a new form of licence whereby a forest company would assume planning and undertake both harvesting and reforestation activities. Negotiations with the forest industry commenced in 1978 and in late 1979 the Crown Timber Act was amended to provide for such arrangements in Forest Management Agreements (FMA's).

With major changes in the north, there was also a shift coming in the south. The lack of assistance and incentives to southern Ontario rural property owners had been a concern to some of the Department's foresters for many years. In 1964 and 1965 staff had conducted a pilot project giving assistance to landowners in four townships in Simcoe County. The trials were successful, particularly in terms of the increase in tree planting, and as a result new legislation—the Woodlands Improvement Act (1966)—allowed the

Minister to enter into agreements with landowners to provide assistance in reforestation and stand improvement, providing the landowner agreed to commit the land to forestry use for 15 years, provide adequate protection, and purchase the trees to be planted. In the first year (1966–67), 3,564 hectares came under agreement[43] and by 1980, 136,984 hectares in 7795 agreements were in place. In addition to Woodlands Improvement Agreements (WIA's) the Ministry increased the advisory services to private woodland owners and by 1974–1975 were dealing with 40,000 enquiries and making over 5,000 field inspections. The number of trees distributed for planting on private lands between 1950 and 1980 ranged from 7 to almost 18 million annually, averaging 12 million. The agreement forests program with Counties and Municipalities begun in 1922, had by 1940 covered only 6,075 hectares, but by 1980 had increased to 109,940 hectares. It was largely through the reforestation taking place on these agreement forests, the plantations established with landowners under the Woodlands Improvement Act, and the smaller areas reforested by other landowners that the forested area of southern Ontario was increased to its present extent.

By 1980, there was a well-developed program for private woodlands in the south and the beginning of a completely new arrangement for forestry on Crown lands in the north, Forest Management Agreements (FMA's). The basic terms of the FMA's were the same for each company. The company agreed to provide forest management plans integrating harvesting and all silvicultural activities, including regeneration, for a 20-year period, subject to Ministry approval, and with an independent review every five years to determine if all requirements had been met. On the basis of the review, if approved, the FMA would be extended a further five years—an 'evergreen' type of arrangement. For the first time in Canada, the FMA company had to provide for public participation during the preparation of each forest management plan. Operating plans described in detail the proposed activities for each five-year period, and annual plans—later called annual work schedules—detailed the forthcoming year.

All plans, forest management (20 years), operating (5 years) and annual had to have Ministry approval. To increase effectiveness of forest management there needed to be a major development in all-weather roads. Additionally, these roads were increasingly being used by the public for access to hunting, fishing and general recreation. Therefore the Ministry, on the basis of a proportion of

Names of Forests

Prior to the FMA's, numbered licences were identified only by the company holding them. In order to give a geographic sense and also emphasize that it is the forest that is the focus of management, each FMA holder was required to name their forest and this is how it would be known officially. Some chose a geographic name, e.g. Spruce River Forest; others chose the name of a person they wished to honour, e.g. Romeo Malette Forest and the Gorden Cosens Forest. The practice of naming forests continued when Sustainable Forest Licences (SFL's) succeeded the FMA's, with the latter retaining their names, and new ones being added to the Crown Management Units on their conversion to SFL's.

Cottonwood

(Populus deltoides)

Located in Chatham, this tree

has a diameter of 265

centimetres with a height of

35.4 metres.

its own roadbuilding costs, paid the FMA holder to construct such roads and maintain them. Further, the Ministry agreed to pay the regeneration costs it (the Ministry) had incurred in the FMA area to the company for regeneration undertaken by the company, and to provide the necessary seed or planting stock. Where a company invested its own money in silvicultural practices that brought about an increase in productivity over that which normally would occur, the increase in volume came at one tenth of the current stumpage rate. Most of the concerns from the industry were for assurance of access to timber on their FMA in the long term, recognizing that, over time, some withdrawals for various purposes would be made by the Crown. For each FMA the Crown agreed that any area withdrawn that exceeded the annual allowable cut area in each 20-year period would have to be replaced by the Crown. Five FMAs were signed in the first year and the most immediate effect was a large increase in demand for planting stock which the Ministry's nurseries could not meet.

By 1980 the Ontario tube had been replaced by larger and more satisfactory containers and, to meet the immediate and projected demand, the Ministry entered into arrangements with a number of private growers in central and northern Ontario to provide container seedlings, primarily to the FMA holders. By 1982–1983 these growers were producing 5.5 million seedlings, the Ministry 11 million container seedlings and 63.6 million bare root stock. Ten years later (1989–1990) after the first agreements were signed, the private growers were shipping 73.5 million seedlings, the Ministry only 5 million containers and 85 million bare root stock. When the Ministry compared[44] the amount of silvicultural activity, in terms of area treated during the first five years of the FMA's with the amount in the preceding five years undertaken by the Ministry, the results were striking. Although the area harvested had increased somewhat, there was a 39 per cent increase in regeneration, a 240 per cent increase in tending of established regeneration, and a 49 per cent increase in site preparation. In effect the FMA program took over from the failed implementation of the Forest Production Policy and, in addition, set in place a continuity by the staff of each of the companies involved which, together with a required monitoring and record system, brought about a major improvement in forest regeneration and its documentation. It is to the credit of the Ministry's forestry staff that by 1980 there was a major body of knowledge and expertise about the silviculture of Ontario's commercial tree species This was recognized by companies within the industry who hired former Ministry staff to assist in their forestry operations.

The accelerated increase in silviculture, in site preparation and regeneration meant that many of the problems associated with these activities posed questions needing research to provide the answers. In 1964, Ontario and Canada signed another joint funding agreement for forest inventory and reforestation under the 1949 Canada Forestry Act. In 1968 they agreed to establish a joint committee, the Canada-Ontario Joint Forest Research Committee (COJFRC) to, *"ensure the most efficient and effective use possible is made of the forestry research resources available in the Ontario Regional Establishment (Canada Forestry Branch) and the Research Branch (Ontario Department of Lands and Forests)"*. The forest industry was not included in committee membership although it could and did participate in field projects.

With the major involvement of industry as forest managers, there was need for a different structure to provide for their direct input in establishing research priorities. From the industry's standpoint these were largely perceived to be set by the research scientists in the two government organizations, too often without consideration of the forest manager's problems.

Photo courtesy Algonquin Provincial Park

1981 to 2000 *F*orests and Urban Society – Forestry's Challenge

Ontario's forests entered the last two decades of the 20th century in a renewed state of recognition. Landowners of private woodlots and managers of public forests were provided with support on a scale that had not previously occurred. In 1982, Agreement Forests[45] celebrated their diamond jubilee at the Hendrie Tract, Simcoe County, and Simcoe County was named the Forest Capital of Canada that year. This honour was bestowed by the Governor General on behalf of the Canadian Forestry Association. Two years later, in 1984, eastern white pine became the official tree of the province.

The results of forest management, particularly reforestation from the 1920s on, gave evidence of what could be achieved in the south. Later, limited management examples from the north were becoming increasingly visible. In addition to the increase in silvicultural treatments of regeneration and tending on each of the FMA areas, a survey of older cutovers which had largely been assumed to be 'not satisfactorily regenerated' (NSR) was made to determine what desired commercial conifer species were present. The results of the survey were surprising: the NSR areas were in the minority, and there were also large areas of old cutover wherein desired conifer regeneration (balsam fir was not a desired species) was established but required tending to release it from brush competition.

One unfortunate feature of the FMA program funding on Crown lands was that as it increased, funding on Crown Forest Management Units failed to increase in the same manner, and actually declined in many instances. By 1988, FMA's covered more than

K. A. Armson

177,293 km² of Crown forest land, or approximately 70 per cent of Crown land under licence.

FMA forest managers had a major concern about the direction of forest research as it pertained to their on-site problems. In 1983, the Ministry undertook a comprehensive review of its research and development operations in forestry, fisheries and wildlife. Before the Committee's report[46] was completed, and as part of the review, the Ministry decided to hold a meeting in November, 1983. Representatives of all client groups, provincial and federal government ministries, universities and the forest industry were asked to attend. There was unanimous agreement about the lack of an effective process to determine research needs and priorities, both provincially and federally, and that client groups had not been involved in any priority-setting.

Two months later (January 1984) there was a further meeting with forestry industry CEOs, university presidents (Guelph, Lakehead and Toronto), and the federal Deputy Minister for Forestry. In April 1984 a group reporting from that meeting recommended that an Ontario Forestry Council (OFC) be formed. The OFC was established by Order-in-Council, October 1984, its purpose to identify research needs and priorities and coordinate all forest research in Ontario. OFC membership consisted of representatives from the forest industry (CEOs), a university president, federal and provincial deputy ministers and two senior officials representing forestry (Ontario) and forest research (Canada).

One of the first actions of the OFC was to determine the amount of funding for forest research and development in Ontario, and how monies were expensed[47]. From 1984–1986, some $9–$10 million was spent annually on research, of which 98 per cent was funded by the federal and provincial agencies (60 per cent federal and 40 per cent provincial). Forty per cent of the total amount was spent equally on tree improvement and forest protection. In addition to monies spent on research, an additional $6 million was spent on technology development.

After conducting this formal survey of needs, perceived priorities and funding, the OFC set up an Ontario Forestry Research Committee (OFRC), headed by the vice chair of the OFC and comprising representatives of provincial and federal research organizations, the universities and forest managers (industry and government). The OFRC actually did the work of reviewing and establishing priorities for the OFC's consideration. Thus, forest industry CEOs were made aware of information about the problems and research needs related to the woodlands—a situation which had not been possible earlier. Once the OFRC was established, all other forestry advisory bodies were disbanded, including the Canada-Ontario Joint Forestry Research Committee (COJFRC). COJFRC had been successful in several projects; one a detailed a long-term study of strip clearcutting in black spruce; another sponsored annual symposia for forest managers and scientists on special topics of interest to both. Responsibility for the continuation of the symposia was assumed by the OFC.

The OFC recommended the creation of a separate, independent Ontario Forest Research Institute funded jointly by the province and the forest industry. By 1990 a memorandum of agreement had been prepared with a projected budget which increased from $3.5 million in 1989–90 (funded entirely by the ministry), to $8 million in 1995–96 (funded 58 per cent by the forest industry and 42 per cent by the ministry). That same year, a new provincial government took power, and the new Minister of Natural Resources (C.J. Wildman) asserted that the proposed institute would represent *"too close a tie to industry,"* and that there was no representation from non-industry groups on its board of directors. OFC Chairman, J.E. Houghton, responded that there was no objection to non-industry representation. The Minister declined to acknowledge this, and stated that his Ministry would be presenting other options. None were forthcoming and the Council came to an end. As of 2001, no joint coordinated structure for establishing forest research needs or setting priorities exists although, regionally, *ad hoc* groups of industry and government persons have formed to deal with specific problem areas—not necessarily of a research nature.

Technology development is important if research findings are to be tested for application in the field. To provide this service, the Ministry set up Technology Development Units (TDU's) during the early 1980s in Timmins, Thunder Bay and Brockville—the latter specifically charged with the development of a Fast Growing Hardwoods program centred on hybrid poplars. During the 1990s, as changes to the Ministry's structure reflected the importance of interdisciplinary projects, the two northern TDU's became the Northeast and Northwest Science and Technology units, respectively. These northern units, and their increase in staff, resulted from a commitment to undertake scientific studies on the impacts of forest management activities, as required by the 1994 Decision

Pin Oak

(Quercus palustris)

Located in Memorial Park, Windsor, this tree has a diameter of 138 centimetres with a height of 27.5 metres.

K. A. Armson

of the Environmental Assessment Board[48].

In addition, a Boreal Science Group was established, along with a research and technology staff at the Centre for Northern Ecosystem Research located at Lakehead University, Thunder Bay.

The Brockville TDU would later be disbanded and replaced by a South Central Science Section with offices at North Bay, and staff situated at other locations throughout southern Ontario.

The provincial government changed in 1985 and the new Minister (Vincent G. Kerrio) appointed Dr. Gordon L. Baskerville, then Dean of Forestry at the University of New Brunswick, to conduct a review (termed an audit[49]), of forest management planning and its implementation on Crown forests in Ontario. Baskerville found the structure of Ontario's forest management to be sound, but he also found severe problems relating to, *"administrative mindset dominating in the Ministry...."* This he believed was exemplified by the Ministry's failure to distinguish between managing the resource and administering its budget. The Ministry prepared an action plan to address Baskerville's concerns, and it did address many of these, but the approaching environmental assessment program overtook the Ministry's efforts.

The Ontario Environmental Assessment Act came into force in 1975; it applied to a wide variety of government activities including management of Crown lands. All activities covered under the Act could be subject to hearings before the Environmental Assessment Board, a quasi-judicial administrative tribunal whose decisions were legally binding unless overturned by the provincial Cabinet.

For several years the Ontario Ministries of Natural Resources and of the Environment held discussions designed to develop the optimum approach to dealing with the forest management activities which occurred in more than 100 management units, over an area of 385,000 km^2. Finally the two agreed that management activities could be placed in one of four major categories: 'access', 'harvesting', 'renewal', and 'maintenance' (tending and protection—including related planning processes). These would be treated as "class" activities, because they were undertakings (such as forest or timber management), which occurred any number of times across a range of geography but with the same attributes, qualities or characteristics. The use of class activities avoided the need for separate assessments not only for each management unit, but for each individual management activity type, a state which would have guaranteed general paralysis of the forestry program

Chinquapin Oak

(Quercus muehlenbergii)

Located near Fanshawe Dam,

London, this tree has a

diameter of 144 centimetres

with a height of 22.6 metres.

on Crown lands for years.

Prior to commencement of the Environmental Assessment hearings of 1988, the Ministry of Natural Resources conducted a series of consultations with a wide range of industry and non-industry groups, including First Nations. It became quite clear from these meetings that many non-industry groups understood "forest management" as administered by the Ministry to include the management of much more than just timber. While there was no dispute that timber management activities could have impacts on many other forest organisms and processes (and indeed this would be what much of the Board's Hearing was about), there was no question that the legislation under which the Forest Resources Group of the Ministry held its mandate was for timber management. As a result, the "Undertaking" for Class Environmental Assessment was for timber, rather than forest management, on Ontario's Crown lands.

This type of assessment was the first of its kind in Ontario, or for that matter in Canada. The Ministry's stated purpose for the undertaking being assessed was, *"to provide a continuous and predictable supply of wood for Ontario's forest products industry."* At the hearings, the Ministry was joined in support, as proponent, by the forest industry; other full-time parties to the hearing, including the Ministry of the Environment, were in opposition. The hearings were held in various locations around the province, beginning in Thunder Bay in May 1988, and continuing, intermittently until 1992—for a total of 411 days.

The Environmental Assessment Board's decision, including 115 terms and conditions was published in April 1994. The Board declared that the Ministry of Natural Resource's assessment was acceptable and that the undertaking of timber management planning was approved. It was, however, in the many terms and conditions that the possible effects on future forests were set out. The Board rejected the notion that some fixed proportion of a managed forest remain without roads; it set out requirements to plan primary roads for a projected 20-year period, with proposals for both primary and secondary roads, presenting alternative locations, while recognizing the impact that each would have on physical and biological components of the landscape, as well as on other users.

One of the major issues was related to harvesting of the forest, particularly the impact of clearcuts. The Board concluded, not only from evidence presented to it, but its own observations during field visits: *"We are persuaded that clearcutting is an acceptable timber management practice, particularly for the boreal forest."* Much of the discussion and debate presented to the board centred on the acceptable size of clearcut and the attributes which a harvested clearcut might share with areas following forest fires. A harvested clearcut does differ from a recently burned forest, but how will it differ over time, and if it does, will the differences (physical or biological) be significant? The Board recognized that this must be the subject of further scientific enquiry and concluded: *"We have little evidence that biological diversity will be maintained or lessened."*

Term and Condition No. 107 specifically directed the Ministry to address biological diversity concerns in timber management planning. The Board stipulated that future clearcuts should not exceed 260 hectares, and that standards for their configuration and contiguity be developed. At the same time it was recognized, for sound biological and or silvicultural reasons, there may be a need to have clearcuts larger than 260 hectares. One example is woodland caribou management undertaken in conjunction with timber harvesting. Given the pattern of forest fires,

Photo courtesy Algonquin Provincial Park

historically to the present, it seems clear that the limit on size for most clearcuts will produce a mosaic patchwork forest patterns on a much smaller scale than those resulting from forest fires alone.

The main purpose of the Ministry's undertaking, to maintain a continuous and predictable supply of wood for the forest industry, came under particular scrutiny and challenge. Ontario's forests, particularly those in the Boreal Region are imbalanced both in amount and age, with older age classes often in preponderance. This imbalance is historical in origin, and has been maintained to some degree by the province's increasingly efficient fire detection and prevention program. As a timber supply forest grows old, its growth rate is reduced and decay increases. In order to bring the forest under management, foresters must harvest its oldest trees (before growth losses become too great) while renewing the area with younger more vigorous trees. There can be no sustained yield from old growth forests in the sense of equal annual amounts; the

Silver Maple

(Acer saccharinum)

Located in Southwold

Township, Elgin County, this

tree has a diameter of 208

centimetres with a height of

32.4 metres.

management challenge is to predict what yield may be given from existing age class distribution, and by various strategies to attempt to move the forest towards a more balanced distribution—the so-called 'normal forest'.

During the 1980s, the Ministry used the existing age class distribution as a basis for determining the 'Maximum Allowable Depletion' (MAD). The MAD determination was then amended at the forest level to take into account local conditions such as accessibility and stand conditions. This approach, was accepted by the Environmental Assessment Board. Since then, more elaborate and sophisticated computer programs have been developed and are being used to assess possible effects of different management strategies on future forest conditions, including yields (annual allowable cuts or AAC's).

On the subject of methods of regeneration, the board concluded that the decision to use natural or artificial methods for forest renewal should be left to the forest manager responsible for each site. In 1984–1986 the Ministry conducted a scientific survey[50] of areas which had been artificially treated by planting or seeding 10 or more years previously (during the 1960s and 1970s). Approximately 80 per cent of these areas achieved the objective of "Free-to-Grow" (FTG)[51] for three commercial conifer species used (jack pine, and black and white spruce); 20 per cent failed to meet the objectives. Whether successful or otherwise, it was clear that other species, be they shrub, herb, or other commercial species—conifer or broadleaved—were also present on these artificially regenerated sites. The board concluded: *"It is a myth that there exists a 'biological desert' of non-regenerating cutovers in our forests."*

Maintenance comprises tending the forest (those activities necessary to ensure that regeneration reaches a Free-to-Grow status, along with subsequent treatments such as thinning to improve growth, quality or both) and protection (ensuring that forest losses due to fire, insects and disease are kept minimal). The Environmental Assessment Board's focus was on the use of chemicals for tending early regeneration, and for the application of pesticides during insect infestations. The fact that both tending and protection materials are usually applied aerially has been a great concern of the public, one particularly conditioned by the reported experiences and use of "agent orange" during the Vietnam war. The Board considered evidence on the safety of chemicals used in

K. A. Armson

tending, and the amounts and frequency of their application, as well as alternatives such as manual cleaning, with all possible effects on wildlife. It concluded that, *"FFT[52] did not convince us that the aerial spraying of herbicides should be prohibited as a tending method. We are persuaded...that aerial spraying of 2,4-D and glyphosate is essential to regenerating conifer stands. FFT failed to convince us that manual tending methods could substitute for aerial spraying."*

On the matter of use of chemicals for insect control, the board took a different position, stating, *"We conclude ... that the aerial spray of chemical insecticides is not essential for pest management purposes in forests of the Area of the Undertaking,"* although the board did accept aerial application of biological pesticides such as B.t. (Bacillus thuringiensis).

The Board dealt with many other items including the manner of public participation in management of the Crown forests, and essentially adopted an industry proposal for such at the forest, regional and provincial levels. It required that a formal Local Citizens Committee (LCC) be established to participate in forest management planning at the forest level. The LCC advises the local Ministry District Manager, and has representation on the planning team for each forest. Along with public participation in FMAs, this requirement for LCCs moved the process of public involvement at the forest level to one well beyond that of most other jurisdictions in Canada or abroad.

What this process has revealed is the relative lack of reliable, accurate and readily understandable information available to the public about forests and their management. One of the important Terms and Conditions (T&C No.86) was the requirement that each management unit be subject to an independent audit every five years, and that this be the basis for extension of Forest Management Agreements, a requirement which was already the practice. What was new was the application of audits to Crown Management Units. When discussing "The Future of Our Forest: new developments and directions," the Board recognized the need for the broadening of forest management to address specific subjects such as 'old growth forests', landscape management and the somewhat illusory matter of 'visual resource management', about which many conflicting views were heard.

It was inevitable given the time-span of the hearing, the large numbers of witnesses, and the amount of evidence presented, that

Locust

(Honey Locust—

Gleditsia triacanthos)

Located north of St. Davids in

the Niagara Region, this tree

has a diameter of 126

centimetres with a height of

25.3metres.

both Ministry and forest industry forest managers would amend existing planning and practices, or adopt new ones perceived to reflect a number of the directions that were presented to the Board.

In 1991, the Minister established The Forest Policy Panel to develop a comprehensive Forest Policy Framework for Ontario. The Panel reported[53] its results in 1993 and in many respects provided substance to concepts of sustainability discussed at the Environmental Assessment Board's Hearings, as well as those included in the 1992 National Forest Strategy[54]. The Panel set a priority agenda for adaptive ecosystem management, improved public participation, and new policies for timber production on Crown land, forest-based tourism, and forest investment and revenue. Such policies would rely on strategic objectives for biodiversity, the maintenance of natural heritage forest lands and the conservation of water, air and soil quality. Together with the Environmental Assessment Board's Decision, the Panel's report provided much of the direction the Ministry would take in the next few years.

The Ontario government had undertaken to review its timber legislation prior to the Board's decision, and in late 1994, assent was given to Bill 171, *An Act to revise the Crown Timber Act to provide for the sustainability of Crown Forests in Ontario*, known generally as the Crown Forest Sustainability Act (CFSA). Previous licences and Forest Management Agreements became Sustainable Forest Licences(SFLs) and the incentives offered to FMA holders were withdrawn. The Minister reassumed absolute authority, as compared with authority under the FMA's with one exception, (for those SFLs granted for terms up to 20 years, provided that the five-yearly review (audit) indicated that the licensee has met the terms and conditions of the licence, *"...the Minister shall, with the approval of the Lieutenant Governor in Council, extend the licence for five years"* [Section 26(4)].).

A continuing concern, one that was echoed by the Environmental Assessment Board was for commitment and continuity of funding support for forest management and regeneration activities on the Crown's public lands. This problem related to the fact that direct revenues, mainly stumpage, paid by industry for Crown timber went to the province's consolidated revenues. It then became a political process to extract, from the provincial coffers, monies for forest management.

Other provinces used different means to short circuit the flow from stump to the provincial treasury by setting up trust accounts into which a portion of the stumpage from each licensee would be paid. The licensee would draw on the trust account to carry out prescribed regeneration or other activities. The rationale was that revenue derived from a specific forest should be returned to the same forest for regeneration.

Following a study in 1994–1995, the Crown dues were revised upward, and the government adopted the principle that annual Crown revenues from stumpage would be separated into three components. One would go directly to a Forest Renewal Trust Fund for use by licensees for regeneration activities. There is a minimum balance maintained in the fund for each forest on which the licensee draws to carry out the necessary renewal activities. This ensures that funding for renewal returns to the forest from which it came. In aggregate, provincially, this minimum balance is approximately $95 million. A second smaller amount, approximately $10 million annually, goes directly to the Forest Futures Trust Fund. This is used for special forestry activities like silvicultural practices for intensive stand management, where forest resources have been destroyed by fire or natural causes, or for other purposes as decided by the Minister. The Ministry or industry licensees can apply for use of the Forestry Futures Trust Fund to the Committee administering the fund. The bulk of the Crown's stumpage, approximately $150 million, continues to find its way into the consolidated revenues of the province. The establishment of trust fund accounts was one way in which the province was able to respond to a major criticism heard at the Environmental Assessment Board's Hearing, about lack of commitment to fund regeneration on Crown lands.

Throughout the 1980s and 1990s, several activist groups focused media and public attention on what they considered harmful logging practices, particularly clearcutting. Associated with this was concern that old growth forests were being destroyed (in Ontario this concern was directed mainly to eastern white and red pine old growth forests, particularly in the Temagami area). As a result, the Minister of Natural Resources established an 'Old Growth Forests Policy Advisory Committee' which made a series of recommendations[55], most of which dealt with process as it pertained to landscape management, protection, forest management, monitoring, education and research. More germane to the issue of "protecting" old growth eastern white and red pines in

Photo courtesy Algonquin Provincial Park

Slippery Elm

(Ulmus rubra)

Located near Bayfield,

this tree has a diameter

of 150 centimetres with

a height of 26.8 metres.

Temagami was the scientific assessment of the dynamics and structure of existing stands in a series of case histories undertaken by Day and Carter[56,57]. They concluded that existing old growth stands were largely established by hot wildfires dating back more than 125 years, and that these stands had also been subject to low intensity understory wildfires since that time. The last hot initiating fire, which resulted in a new pine forest, in the Temagami area was in 1864. Since the early 1900s, fire protection has precluded those hot initiation fires which were the basis of today's existing old stands. Fire rotation—as distinct from normal forest biological rotation, essentially stand rotation prior to 1912—was 125 years; since that date it has been extended to 1200 years. Thus past fire prevention and any effort to "protect" these old pine stands, has permitted the reproduction of tolerant species like red maple, balsam fir and other hardwoods which now occupy the area and will, eventually, succeed the pines.

Examination of the Lake Temagami Skyline Reserve bears testimony to this fact, as well as providing evidence that specific silvicultural treatments like clearcutting and the shelterwood system can be used to manage and sustain a balanced eastern white and red pine forest with appropriate distribution of age classes including "old growth."

Historically, today's old growth stands of pine are an anomaly which has developed since the early 1900s; they did not occur before human intervention. By continuing present non-intervention practices, we are guaranteeing the essential replacement of pines by other species with lesser biological rotation ages, less visual appeal, greater susceptibility to major insect depredations, and a totally different set of ecological conditions.

Undoubtedly, individual trees and small groves of very old pines occurred in the past, especially on isolated rocky crags or other locations which successive fires either missed or only lightly burned. Representative examples of these conditions and trees will always be with us, but they should not be confused with the key issue of how to manage the larger forests in which eastern white pine and red pine should be sustained.

Concern by many public groups and individuals about forestry practices and old growth are symptomatic of a broader dissatisfaction relating to the matter of land use designation. During the 1970s, the Ministry of Natural Resources engaged in a protracted process of land use planning which culminated in the early 1980s

K. A. Armson

in the Strategic Land Use Plans (SLUP's) at the regional level, and within the context of those plans, District Land Use Guidelines (DLUG's). There was no formal public involvement in this process, and two broad groups of individuals who had particular interests in Crown forest lands were for the most part unsatisfied with the outcomes: those whose livelihood was dependent on forest resources other than timber (tourist operators, trappers, fishers and hunters who generally lived in the forest area), and recreationists, canoeists, bird watchers, hikers and others who seek enjoyment in those forests that either have not been accessed for timber, or in which logging has occurred but the signs of past activities are not readily evident. Numerically, this latter group was largely urban-based. Their use of the forest was transient or periodic in nature.

Although the concerns and issues related to conflicts, real or perceived, over land use designation for timber management were at the heart of much of the debate during the Hearing of the Environmental Assessment Board, questions as to whether or not an area should be designated a park or wilderness were not part of the discussion. The Board believed, *"our authority to provide conditions of approval is related to issues of land use generally."* This was evident from the Board's Term and Condition No.34 which required for each timber management plan, that selection criteria and optional areas for harvest be provided by the Ministry to the public at the beginning of the planning cycle. Such "land use planning" is at a scale and time period—5 years—which is quite different from that generally considered at a regional or provincial level in the establishment of parks. The Board did consider, however, those land use values that would be present within the timber management unit—wildlife habitats, trap-line areas and so forth.

By 1997, the Ministry of Natural Resources, in conformance with general government direction, had removed itself entirely from operational silvicultural activities on Crown lands licenced to companies. In so doing it gave those companies added responsibilities in planning, inventory and monitoring. At the same time, the Ministry began to withdraw from operational activities on Crown Management Units and initiated the process of their conversion to Sustainable Forest Licences (SFL's). The Minister of Natural Resources still retained regulatory authority over planning and operations through the use of an approval procedure and the conduct of audits for compliance purposes. Increasingly, the setting

Beech

(American Beech—

Fagus grandifolia)

Located in the Springwater

Cons. Area, Elgin County,

this tree has a diameter of

92 centimetres with

a height of 17.7 metres.

aside of productive forests on SFL areas from harvesting and other management activities resulted in major concerns by the forest industry, which was concerned for both current and foreseeable fibre supplies, as well as the long-term prospects of utilizing timber from more recently regenerated forests (resulting from the companies' silvicultural efforts).

The broader issues of land use would become the focus of the Lands for Life program in 1997—a *"new comprehensive land-use planning process that strikes a balance between **protection and use** of Ontario's natural resources."*[58] The government had three initiatives it wished to implement: i) the creation of more parks and protected areas; ii) a resource-based tourism policy; and iii) forest management.

The process consisted of establishing three regional round tables—Boreal West, Boreal East and Great Lakes – St. Lawrence. Each involved representation from a wide range of interested parties, and each was charged with preparing recommendations regarding areas for protection, resource use-needs, basic conditions for compatible use, and targets and indicators to determine the long-term health of the resources. The Ministry had determined at the outset, that there would be 27 new parks and conservation reserves created, with more added in the future.

Following the round table reports in 1998, the Ministry of Natural Resources developed a Proposed Land Use Strategy, which it termed the Living Legacy. Two features of the Living Legacy which had not existed in previous land-use designations and which resulted directly from the round tables were the designation of Enhanced Management Areas (EMA's), and the provision for Resource Stewardship Agreements (RSA's). Within the former, resource management activities, including forestry, might be permitted but with conditions on timing, location, method and access, in recognition of values related to natural heritage, recreation, remote access, fish and wildlife, Great Lakes coastal areas, resource-based tourism and intensive forestry. The latter (RSA's) provided for agreements (for example) between a resource-based tourism operator and a sustainable forest licence holder to establish the nature, timing or other arrangements for such forest management activities as may be undertaken to the satisfaction of both parties within a given area.

The issue of increased land for parks and conservation protection areas was a particularly difficult one, because it had to be done at the expense of existing productive forest areas already under sustainable forest licences to the forest industry. Simultaneously with the release of the Living Legacy report, the Ministry, the Partnership for Public Lands (the World Wildlife Fund Canada, the Federation of Ontario Naturalists and the Wildlands League), as well as representatives from three forest companies met to determine a mutually acceptable approach for withdrawal of productive forest lands from industry while taking into account industry needs.

The document resulting from this meeting specified 31 elements about which the parties agreed, and was formally termed the Forest Accord. There were two basic premises: i) no net increase in the cost of wood delivered to a mill, and ii) no net reduction in fibre supply. It was also clear that the immediate objective of placing 12 per cent of the Crown lands subject to the withdrawal would be only a base level which would increase over time. In 1999, the Ontario government announced a $30 million Living Legacy Trust Fund to be used over a five-year period to implement the intent of the Forest Accord.

Overall, the result of reducing the area of Ontario's forests subject to forest management activities (whether the primary objective is timber production or not) will be that our forests will be less disturbed by planned manipulation, although natural disturbances will still occur. In aggregate the province's forests will become older than those prior to the presence of Europeans since the 17th century.

Photo courtesy Algonquin Provincial Park

Algonquin Hotel, Algonquin Park, 1934–1936.

Photo courtesy Province of Ontario Ministry of Natural Resources

K. A. Armson

VI

Changing Values and Future Forests

Ontario's forests developed as a result of a series of events, which had either a regional or continental impact. Climatic change, for example, occurred over hundreds, if not thousands of years. Other episodic events, like severe ice storms or exceptional warm periods might occur during the middle of a single winter. Long-term climatic change has a significant impact on any forest, such effects are usually imperceptible during the human lifespan. Effects of episodic change, however, are highly visible depending on species, composition, and local conditions. A forest's general nature is determined by the broad climatic spectrum of conditions which occur over the centuries. Within that canopy—which itself is always changing— the physiography of a forest's landscape provides a second range of conditions and opportunities for both plants and animals to develop, and to form the communities and forest types that we as humans come to recognize, identify, categorize and use.

At the landscape level, other, more immediate factors cause significant changes in the forest which are readily apparent: fires, floods, insects, diseases, and attacks from other organisms. We usually link these results to their occurrence in different situations, building from these links our conceptions of how the forest conditions we see today come to be; our reasoning is based on objectively observed features, on information gained from other sources about similar conditions, and on the cultural and societal milieu in which we live.

Ontario's early Aboriginal inhabitants forged a special relationship with the land and its forests because of their hunting and fishing; these elements formed the basis of much of Aboriginal mythology. The Late Woodland Indians developed an agriculture

Lyons Creek Oak

In the cemetery of Lyons Creek United Church, Niagara Falls stands a beautiful white oak measuring 24 metres in height with d.b.h. of 143 centimetres. This oak is said to have been present when the first church on the site was built in 1806.

based economy, and were aware of the importance of trees in their environment.

Early European settlers came to Ontario from cultural backgrounds which often had no relevance to the forest conditions in their new home. Some may have been influenced by the often fictional accounts created as inducements to immigrate. Some may have perceived North American forests as dark, evil, and menacing—home to such threatening creatures as wolves. A homesteading family living in relative isolation, would also make up such stories to deter their children from wandering into the woods.

Nevertheless, forests were an obstacle to early settlement, agricultural development and manufacturing, all of which were to be the foundation of Ontario's economy. Major public ownership of forests coupled with demands for timber, either as a result of wars or industrial development elsewhere, meant that exploitation of the forests needed to be organized so that entrepreneurs, governments and hence society, benefited. Two primary conflicting sets of values emerged: one valued only the land, wherein its timber and other components were incidental; the second valued essentially only the standing timber, with the value of the land being incidental.

These two determinations guided Ontario's forestry policies throughout the 19th century, and into the early 1900s. Some lumbermen, with vested interests in a continuing supply of timber and a few far-sighted individuals, who could see the need for conservation, realized that simple exploitation was not sustainable in the long run. However, it was concern for the water supply to Ontario's streams and rivers, which was vital to the major transportation routes, which resulted in studies and action.

Witness the rationales for the establishment of Algonquin Park in 1883 and the Trent Valley survey of 1912. Protection from fire was an initial concern because of the impact in destroying valuable timber; only later, with development of agricultural settlements in the northern forests, did protection of human lives and property become most important.

Introduction of professional and scientific approaches to the management of Ontario's forests (primarily for timber, but also for water conservation, wildlife habitat, and even aesthetics) began in the early 1900s, with the founding of two organizations. A group of senior businessmen and civil servants started the Canadian Forestry Association (CFA) in 1900. In 1907 the first professional

K. A. Armson

school of forestry was established at the University of Toronto.

Sir Henry Joly de Lotbinière, the first Chairman of the CFA, stated the five main objectives of that Association at its inaugural meeting[1]: protect the forests from fire; foster the public awareness of the dangers of forest destruction on water conservation; recommend the division of public lands into agricultural, timber and mineral areas to prevent settlement on forest lands unsuited to agriculture but capable of sustaining tree crops; promote tree planting in the treeless prairies and on streets and in parks of villages, towns and cities; inform the public about forestry.

Although these objectives reflected the values of the CFA, they had no connection with Ontario's grass roots public or with the politicians of the time. Indeed, as railway access through the north increased, expansion and development were the hallmarks of the early 1900s. The 1920s brought a limited beginning of professional planning and forest management, but this was directed almost exclusively to growing timber in an economic context and providing basic information about the forests.

The early cadre of university-trained foresters gave their attention to the formation of a professional body, the Canadian Society of Forest Engineers (CSFE), which was established in 1908 to consider and discuss, *"technical subjects relating to the theory and practice of forestry, and to cultivate an esprit de corps among members of the profession"*[2]. In 1950 the CSFE became the Canadian Institute of Forestry-Institut Forestier du Canada, with sections throughout Canada, including Ontario.

Provincially, a number of prominent foresters believed that there should be a single professional body to represent Ontario foresters. In 1957 the Ontario Professional Foresters Association (OPFA) was established by legislation as a registration body. Since then, the OPFA has been active in many areas, but its voluntary membership creates limitations. The OPFA cannot apply professional standards of practice to non-members, be they foresters or others purportedly practising forestry. With the rapid increase in silviculture and other forestry practices on both public and private lands, and the potential environmental impact of these activities, there has been a growing need for the OPFA to become a licensing body for closer regulation of professional forestry practitioners and public protection from unprofessional practices. Legislation (Bill 110) to bring this about was introduced into the Ontario legislature in mid 2000 and received Royal Assent in October of that year.

Photo courtesy Algonquin Provincial Park

Ritson Pear

Just off Ritson Road north of Highway 401, Oshawa, stands a large and productive pear tree. According to local historians and the Ontario Ministry of Agriculture and Food, Mrs. John Ritson planted seeds from a pear sent to her from Boston, Massachusetts in the early 1800s. This tree is believed to be an original of that cultivar.

During the 1920s, road and water access, and the establishment of resorts for city folk (not only from Ontario but also from the United States) introduced a set of values no less economic than timber. An educated urban clientele was interested in the wilderness and the scenic values of the forest as long as it also provided good fishing and civilized amenities in the lodges and hotels where the vacationers stayed. Concurrent with these developments was the establishment of summer camps for youth. These increased the consciousness of emotional sensitivity towards wilderness values at a young age. These shifting viewpoints created little conflict along the Georgian Bay, into the Muskokas, and in Algonquin Park.

In the Temagami[3] area, however, mining interests and changes in water levels resulting from dams created a problem. There was also concern about the visual appearance of the area's forests when viewed from Lake Temagami. In 1935 a "Skyline" reserve was established, which covered the region from the Temagami shoreline to the top of its surrounding ridges. Timber had been cut years before behind this area, as it had throughout the Georgian Bay area. Logging operations occurred during the winter and were essentially out-of-sight and therefore out-of-mind. It was in these areas, and the Quetico area of northwestern Ontario, that major confrontations over timber and non-timber values occurred during the latter half of the 1900s.

Up until the 1950s, values that had existed for the past century or more were those that governed the administration, planning and activities in Ontario's public forest lands. The forests we have today reflect the results of actions during that period. The actual forest extent has changed little in northern and central Ontario; in southern Ontario the cover has increased with few major exceptions, as in the extreme southwest.

The nature of Ontario's northern boreal forest has changed in several respects; today upland mixedwoods usually have much lower proportions of spruce and pine, while the poplar and balsam fir populations have increased. The jack pine forest is increasing, largely as a result of the successful regeneration of harvested or burned jack pine forest areas during the past 40 years.

Lowland black spruce has regenerated relatively well both under the seasonal logging for pulpwood as practiced before mechanized harvesting, and more recently, with harvesting methods which minimize damage to any advanced young spruce trees. During the early period of mechanized logging of black spruce on

K. A. Armson

wet soils, regeneration was less successful or delayed; sometimes tamarack replaced the spruce.

Upland black spruce, often on shallow soils, was initially difficult to regenerate. Originally these stands regenerated naturally as a result of forest fires, but without some form of disturbance additional to logging, they were less successful. Since the 1980s, combinations of strip clearcutting, with prescribed site preparation and regeneration practices, have ensured that spruce can be maintained on these sites.

Increasing amounts of old age classes, although variable within the northern forest, are a result of rapid fire detection and suppression, and the setting aside of significant areas within the productive forest for 'protection' (where forest management is excluded or severely limited).

Remote tourism is another factor affecting central and northern forest areas. For much of the 1900s, this was based on fly-in camps. In addition to the lure of good hunting and fishing, one of the inducements of this phenomenon has been the sense of 'wilderness'. The client group is largely urban-based, and has historically come from Canadian centers, and more importantly from affluent areas of the eastern and midwestern United States. More recently, this industry has begun to attract Europeans.

During the latter half of the 1900s, particularly the last two decades, the sight, from the air, of large scale harvesting of the boreal forest has created tension between the forest industry and tourist operators. Further tensions developed when large numbers of hunters and fishermen used forest roads into areas hitherto considered the preserve of tourist camp operators. Increased public access led to deferments and rescheduling of forest management activities in those forest areas where tourist establishments were active.

The net result of these conflicting demands on Ontario's forests means a more fragmented forest structure than that which occurred earlier, when the only significant natural disturbance was from fire. In addition, present-day areas of generally less than 250 hectares (considered small areas), which are harvested and then regenerated, create a "postage stamp" mosaic of new forest stands. These are usually a hundred–fold times smaller (or more) than previous forest stands resulting from wildfire.

Today's society wishes to see large areas of natural wilderness, but, paradoxically, also wants managed forests to come in small

Norway Spruce

(Picea abies)

On a front lawn in Owen Sound, is an unusual Norway spruce with a diameter of 66 centimetres and a height of nearly 20 metres. Forming a circle around the tree are some twenty-nine offspring of varying heights with diameters of 5 to 30 centimetres.

compartment-sized units; the result is a significant visual change in the future landscape, with concomitant changes in its ecological features, particularly as they relate to wildlife habitats. Forest managers are endeavouring to address visual and ecological values by planning the locations, shapes and nature of cutovers, and their regeneration boundaries. It is, however, ultimately the scale and context of the larger landscape which determines how well such values may be maintained in the long-term.

The main factor affecting the Great Lakes – St. Lawrence Forest region of central Ontario over the past 150 years has been the reduction in amount of eastern white and red pines following logging, particularly in those upland locations where these trees grew mixed with broadleaved species. Generally, the pines regenerated naturally on the drier, coarser-textured soils. They were often not cut when they occurred on very shallow sites over bedrock, either because they were inaccessible for logging, or because they were too small. Currently, the future of eastern white pine is assured in those areas where it is being managed, primarily by the shelterwood silvicultural system with suitable site preparation. In upland poor quality broadleaved forests, white pine can be reintroduced successfully, but only by a costly combination of silvicultural practices: clearcutting, severe site preparation, planting and tending. Red pine is more difficult to regenerate, and often has to be planted. There will likely be fewer future forests of naturally regenerated red pine.

Only minimal management of eastern hemlock presently occurs and this is related mainly to maintaining deer yards for winter cover. Many hemlock stands in central Ontario were killed during the early 1900s when they were girdled to obtain bark for tanning. The trees were often left standing instead of being cut for timber. Large-scale logging for quality hardwoods in this forest region did not begin until the 1930s; veneer quality yellow birch was the most desired species. After World War II and until the 1970s, other hardwoods, especially sugar maple, were logged selectively for the best timber. The residual broadleaved forests consisted of lower quality, poorly formed trees. Today, these 'degraded' forests extend over large areas. Tree-marking programs to improve and manage them, under a form of selection silvicultural system, have been in effect for the past 20 years, and are now showing success. Such programs are mandatory on Crown forests and are undertaken by the forest companies managing these

K. A. Armson

forests. Some companies provide similar services to private woodland owners from whom they purchase timber. One of the major
reasons for the selective highgrading of the hardwoods in this
region has been the lack of markets for poorer quality material.
Although this changed to some degree during the latter quarter of
the 1900s, it still remains an impediment to more intensive
management.

Recreational uses and cottage development throughout the
central Ontario region, especially since the 1950s, have brought a
large number of people to the province's forests, mainly from
southern parts of Ontario. Much of the public use of this area was
originally seasonal, but increased leisure time, year-round use of
properties, and access with trail machines and snowmobiles has
changed public perception of the forest. Recreational users see their
values best protected by maintaining the existing forest rather than
subjecting it to management for timber; in the long run, however
timber management may be the only way the public's forests and
their associated values may be maintained.

A satisfactory consensus is required
between forest managers and the public at the
local forest level so that Ontario's forests can
be properly managed, and the desired values
maintained; this consensus needs to be developed in a spatial and temporal framework of
the entire forest, not in a series of static locations. Wildlife habitats provide many
examples of change; when the nature of each
habitat changes, the forests in which they
occur develop and change too. Sometimes
desired conditions may only be present for a
few years, as in young regenerating forests;

Photo courtesy Algonquin Provincial Park

habitats in older stands may be present over many decades. Forests
grow old and change in nature and structure without necessarily
sustaining the values we presently associate with them.

Although there are large tracts of privately-owned forest lands
in the Boreal and Great Lakes – St. Lawrence forest regions, the
predominant ownership is public, as Crown lands. Limited public
participation in Ontario Crown land forest management began in
1980. Since 1994, the formation of Local Citizens Committees
(LCC's) has been mandated for all Crown land forests under
Sustainable Forest Licences (SFL's). In these Committees, the

Sweetgum

The Port Dover Cemetery has four mature sweetgum trees (Liquidambar styraciflua). The largest has a d.b.h. of 90 centimetres. According to the caretaker, Elijah Doan planted these trees shortly after his arrival from Pennsylvania in 1806.

implications of present and planned future forest management practices in determining the nature of the forests they create will become better understood. Today's desired values should be placed in that context.

The total extent of southern Ontario's forests has increased during the past century. This increase occurred almost exclusively on the areas that were cleared for agriculture in the 1800s and early 1900s. Some lands were revegetated as a result of natural encroachment of herbaceous vegetation, shrubs and trees. In many instances, especially areas of lesser vegetation and shrubs, there has been a significant component of naturalized introduced (non-native) species, forming early successional stages, which ultimately are replaced by native species. Structures of these forests are usually uneven, as residuals of the alien species persist in openings—as for example, the shrub buckthorn which now occupies some old fields which are hardwood forests today.

In other instances, depending on the last agricultural use and type of location, a forest may be invaded over a relatively short period by a single species. Eastern white-cedar stands on old pastures are common. There are thousands of hectares of eastern redcedar on abandoned dry farmland over limestone bedrock in eastern Ontario. As these stands mature, they will open up, allowing other, more shade tolerant tree and shrub species to become established.

Another major cause of the increase in southern Ontario's forests has been the active reforestation program implemented by the province under agreements with municipalities, conservation authorities, and individual landowners. Because of the well-drained upland nature of much of the lands being planted, conifers such as eastern white and red pines, and white and Norway spruce have predominated.

Scots pine was introduced more than a hundred years ago and remained popular as a Christmas tree during the middle and late 1900s. Unfortunately, the European seed sources for most of the Ontario Scots pine plantations produced trees of poor form, rapid growth and ready regeneration. Many of these plantations have little timber value and, although destruction is desirable, their extirpation is a costly process.

With age and appropriate management, plantations of single species such as red pine, once reviled as "biologically sterile," have become forests of considerable diversity in plant and animal

K. A. Armson

species, in addition to being valuable recreational uses. This is typical of the county, regional and Conservation Authority forests established as Agreement Forests beginning in 1922. For the most part these forests are still professionally managed—but with the goal of maintaining non-timber values, as well as conserving the timber value.

Broadleaved forests of the southern Great Lakes – St. Lawrence and Deciduous regions were largely fragmented as a result of settlement. Many farm woodlots have been selectively highgraded over the years with a resultant increase in poor quality trees. Other woodlots have been used for pasture, wherein the forests have been degraded with minimal regeneration and a reduction in quality of existing trees. Various government programs provided marketing advice and assistance to owners, placing emphasis on better control over the cutting on woodlots. The result has been a significant improvement in woodlot quality, although there is still much to be done.

Values and uses of forests are human determinations. The manner in which we attempt to sustain our forests is dependent on human activities, primarily those of forest management. Professionally and technically, we are aware of most of the necessary forest management planning and practices to achieve the values and forest uses society desires. Why then is there so much concern and conflict about Ontario's forests? The answer is complicated:

- The historical pattern of exploitative development of public forest lands is still perceived, erroneously, as common practice.
- Forest management during the past several decades was directed essentially to the production of timber, with variable concern for other values and uses.
- Government's management of public forest lands has been characterized more by administrative concerns than by commitment to continuity and accountability in forest management.
- The public's view of forest values and use has been expressed largely in terms of protecting single purpose, static and exclusive forest areas in reserves rather than as an integration into the management of the forest as a whole.

Basswood

(Tilia americana)

Located in Dungannon

Township, Hastings

County, this tree has

a diameter of

189 centimetres with

a height of 23 metres.

The result has been that as forest management has progressed, particularly during the past 30 years, the resultant achievements have been limited because of constraints on appropriate activities. Ontario needs to develop a forest management goal which contains a clear definition of the values and uses that society wants future forests to provide, coupled with the recognition that these values and the resultant forests will change with time.

The values we now place on forests are those of an urban rather than a rural society. Ours is a society which has put a premium on having trees on streets, in parks and in the country-side. In the urban setting, the need to manage trees in order to maintain desired values is acknowledged and this task is undertaken by urban forestry staff in our major cities. Similar recognition generally does not carry over into the larger forest areas of the province. The concept of forest management involving production of timber with a commercial value is either qualified or unacceptable, even although such production can be demonstrated to be the most appropriate and often only way to conserve other non-timber values.

Agreement Forests (counties, regions and Conservation Authorities) where recreational use is high, require forest management to achieve non-timber values together with the production of commercial timber. Both can occur successfully. In many of these forests, timber values contribute significantly to the forests' revenues. If we can extend this acceptance to the larger area of Crown forests, currently excluded as reserves without any form of forest management, then the public of Ontario will benefit and our forests will be maintained in a healthy state. This does not mean that there should not be significant park areas where non-human forces can be left to determine the state of the forest. It should mean that other non-commercial uses of Ontario's forest, such as recreation be excluded or rigidly controlled.

The issue of fire control in Ontario's wilderness areas is one that has to be decided on a specific basis. It is a key issue, one that can argued from different points of view. Purists would like to see fires left to burn, but because fires do not recognize human-defined boundaries, this places adjacent properties, values, and possibly lives at risk. A forest management approach would use prescribed fires to obtain similar results to those occurring from natural forest fires.

K. A. Armson

Forest management is necessary for sustaining the values that society places on its forests. Manipulation of a forest structure by conventional and proven silvicultural practices is the only effective way to do this. The degree and nature of that management is dependent on two intertwined marketplaces. One is that of society as a whole; the other is of the timber and non-timber resource products that a forest can produce. Society usually places high non-monetary values on the benefits and relatively little value on the costs of management.

It is the marketplace for products and services that generates the significant revenues which will provide for meaningful forest management. The production of timber either as a primary objective or as a by-product in the management for other values makes sense, ecologically, economically and socially. When the majority of Ontario's citizens realize this, and as owners of their natural resources commit through their governments to this goal, then the future of Ontario's forests is assured.

Photo courtesy Algonquin Provincial Park

VII

Forest Facts

The Land Base

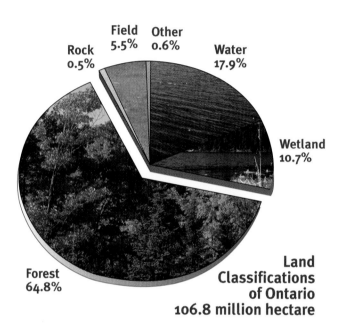

Rock
0.5%

Field
5.5%

Other
0.6%

Water
17.9%

Wetland
10.7%

Forest
64.8%

Land Classifications of Ontario
106.8 million hectare

Land Class	Areas in thousands ('000's) of hectares
Water – inland	10,175.3
Water – Great Lakes	8,886.9
Wetland – marsh/bog/fen	11,418.3
Wetland – forested – treed bog and fen	14,169.2
Conifer forest (softwoods)	23,817.4
Broadleaved forest (hardwoods)	8,586.0
Mixedwood forest	15,421.5
Disturbed forest – fire and harvested	7,280.8
Rock	548.3
Field and Agriculture	5,854.2
Other – roads, towns, cities etc	641.9
Total	106,800.0

1 Forested—Productive and Non-Productive Lands by Ownership
Areas in thousands ('000's) of hectares

Class	Ontario Crown			Federal	Private	Total
Forested	**Parks & Reserves**	**Other**	**Total**			
Productive	4,570	29,032	33,602	484	5,527	39,613
Non-Productive (muskeg, brush, rock)	582	4,782	5,364	64	644	6,072
Totals	5,152	33,814	38,966	548	6,171	45,685

2 Forested Lands by Ownership
Areas in thousands of hectares

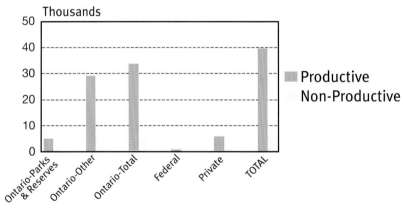

Source: Ontario Ministry of Natural Resources

Inventoried Forest Lands—Ownership

N.B. Of the total area of the province (106,800,000 hectares), 59,715,181 hectares are included in the Forest Resources Inventory (FRI), 1996, as up-dated in 1999, and form the basis for the data in these tables. The area not included in the FRI is that of the Northern Boreal forest and Barrens north of a line approximately from 500 N at the Ontario-Québec border to 520 N at the Ontario-Manitoba border.

K. A. Armson

Inventoried Forest Lands—Age Classes

Areas of Conifer (Softwood) Forest by Age Classes

Areas in thousands ('000's) of hectares

Age Class 20 yr. classes	Ontario Crown			Federal	Private	Total
	Parks & Reserves	Other	Total			
0–20	266.6	3593.8	3860.4	18.6	469.9	4348.9
21–40	132.5	1422.4	1554.9	8.7	147.3	1710.9
41–60	434.0	2747.0	3181.0	30.2	378.6	3589.8
61–80	553.3	3729.0	4282.3	58.4	477.4	4818.1
81–100	476.4	3266.1	3742.5	59.1	253.4	4055.0
101–120	394.9	2542.4	2937.3	23.7	105.9	3066.9
121–140	385.9	2123.0	2508.9	10.6	77.6	2597.1
141–160	414.1	1492.7	1906.8	8.7	42.7	1958.2
161–180	72.5	275.3	347.8	1.1	6.6	355.5
180+	15.5	47.7	63.2	0.3	1.5	65.0

Gross Total Volumes—millions of cubic metres

Conifer	382.9	2832.0	3214.9	33.4	248.2	3496.5

Mean Annual Increment—thousands of cubic metres per year

Conifer	4483.3	33783.6	38266.9	416.7	3574.1	42257.7

Conifer (Softwood) Age Classes by Ownership

Areas in thousands of hectares

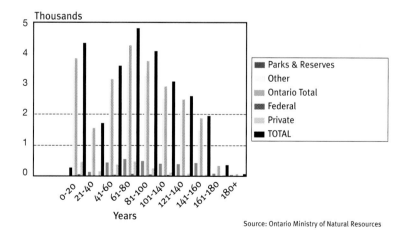

Source: Ontario Ministry of Natural Resources

Inventoried Forest Lands—Age Classes

Areas of Broadleaved (Hardwood) Forest by Age Classes
Areas in thousands ('000's) of hectares

Age Class 20 yr. classes	Ontario Crown			Federal	Private	Total
	Parks & Reserves	Other	Total			
0–20	56.1	589.3	645.4	12.8	1103.9	1762.1
21–40	93.8	523.1	616.9	21.1	359.4	997.4
41–60	307.4	1524.9	1832.3	55.3	907.0	2794.6
61–80	399.6	2345.4	2745.0	91.0	1052.5	3888.5
81–100	287.4	1584.4	1871.8	58.2	543.7	2473.7
101–120	123.3	740.5	863.8	20.9	134.9	1019.6
121–140	48.0	264.9	312.9	3.7	17.3	333.9
141–160	50.8	163.8	214.6	1.5	5.9	222.0
161–180	38.4	41.2	79.6	0.1	0.5	80.2
180+	20.5	12.7	33.2	0	0	33.2

Gross Total Volumes—millions of cubic metres

Broadleaved	202.9	1389.2	1592.1	31.2	479.1	2102.4

Mean Annual Increment—thousands of cubic metres per year

Broadleaved	2583.1	18610.2	21193.3	440.0	7142.9	28776.2

Broadleaved (Hardwood) Age Classes by Ownership

Areas in thousands of hectares

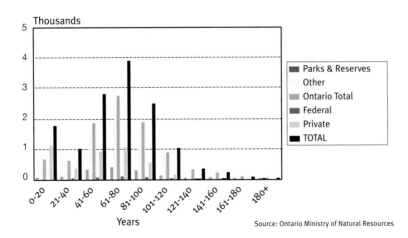

Source: Ontario Ministry of Natural Resources

K. A. Armson

Broadleaved Age Classes - All Ownerships

Areas of Intolerant & Tolerant Forests in thousands of hectares
Intolerant (poplars, birches etc.); Tolerant (maples, beech etc.)

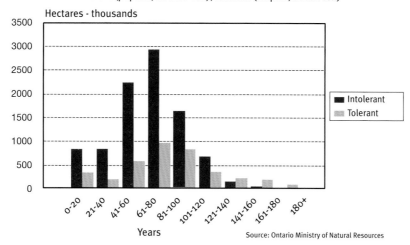

Hectares - thousands

■ Intolerant
▨ Tolerant

Years

Source: Ontario Ministry of Natural Resources

Boreal Forest Region

Main Species' Working Groups
Areas as Percent of Total WG's

black spruces 53.6%

Jack pine 17.0%

others 3.4%

white birch 7.4%

poplar 13.7%

balsm fir 4.8%

Source: Ontario Ministry of Natural Resources

Great-Lakes-St. Lawrence & Deciduous Forest Regions

Main Species' Working Groups
Areas as Percent of Total WG's

black & white spruces 7.1%

sugar maple 24.7%

Jack pine 7.8%

white & red pines 8.0%

white birch 9.2%

other broadleaved 9.9%

poplar 19.9%

other conifers 13.5%

Source: Ontario Ministry of Natural Resources

A Working Group consists of the aggregate of all stands having the same predominant species and managed under a similar silvicultural system.

VIII

About the Author

Ken Armson is a professional forester who has spent more than 50 years in teaching, research, policy and administration in forestry. As a professor of forestry at the University of Toronto for 26 years he taught and conducted research in forest soils and silviculture. In 1975–76 he undertook a major study of forest management in Ontario for the Ministry of Natural Resources. As a result of his report's recommendations he joined the Ministry in 1978 to develop Forest Management Agreements, whereby forest companies assumed full responsibility for forest planning, harvesting and regeneration. From 1979 to 1986 he was successively Chief Forester and Executive Coordinator for the province's forestry program, and in 1986 became Provincial Forester. He has been involved in public education about forestry throughout his career, working with the Ontario Forestry Association on teachers' courses and programs on natural resources management. During 1988–1990, he was a witness in the Environmental Assessment of Ontario's timber management on Crown lands, and after leaving the Ministry in 1989 he has worked as a forestry consultant. Since 1994 he has been engaged in the development and application of the CSA International's Sustainable Forest Management standard, and is a member of the Technical Committee responsible for the standard. He is the author of texts on nursery soil management, forest soils and most recently a book on Canadian forests for teachers.

List of Tables

List of Figures

XI

Glossary

Alvar	a vegetation type which occurs on shallow limestone areas subject to drought and frequent fires
Biodiversity	a general term used to describe the complexity of ecosystems, species richness and genetic variation
Board foot	the amount of wood in an unfinished board one foot long, one foot wide and one inch thick; used in estimating the volume of sawtimber in standing trees and expressed usually in thousands 'foot board measure'(fbm)
Chicot	dead standing trees commonly left after forest fires
Clinal	variation in a species, usually along a geographic gradient
Clone	genetically identical individuals usually derived by asexual reproduction from a common ancestor
Drumlin	'whale-back' shaped hills formed during the advance of a glacier, their long axes orientated in the direction of ice flow. Drumlins are often found in groups called "drumlin fields"
Ecosystem	a general term usually referring to the complex of living and non-living components and processes in a specific situation

Eskers	sinuous ridges of deposits of sands and gravels left by streams that flowed within a glacier
Evapotranspiration	the combined amount of water lost as vapour from soil and water surfaces and vegetation
Forest Floor	the organic materials overlying the upper surface of mineral soil
Igneous	rocks formed from the cooling and solidification of once hot fluid material originating in the earth's interior
Kames	hills of stratified sands and gravels, often conical, formed at the edge of melting glaciers
Isostatic uplift	the upward movement of the earth's crust resulting from the removal of a large mass of glacial ice
Lacustrine	deposits, primarily silt and clay particles which settled out in large bodies of water such as lakes
Laccolith	a large dome-shaped formation on the earth's crust, usually comprising metamorphic rock
Layerings	an individual plant originating from a another plant's branch which has developed roots after contact with the soil or other media
Litter	the surface layer of the forest floor, composed of relatively undecomposed organic materials such as leaves, twigs, stems, bark and fruits
Mast	the fruit of trees or shrubs which are a food for wildlife or livestock
Metamorphic	rocks which have undergone chemical or physical change since their original formation
Moder	a type of forest humus which is transitional between mor and mull humus types
Mor	a type of poorly decomposed humus, often matted, which accumulates on the

K. A. Armson

	soil surface and is clearly differentiated from the underlying mineral soil
Moraine	unsorted and sorted materials left by glaciers during their advance or retreat (ground moraine), at the margin (terminal or end moraine), or between two lobes of the glacier (interlobate moraine)
Mull	a type of humus which is well-decomposed and incorporated in the upper mineral soil
Oriented Strand Board	a type of waferboard in which the wafers are oriented in direction
Outwash	sand and gravel deposited by melting water from a glacier in terraces or broad fans
Peneplain	an extensive area of relatively low relief resulting from long-term erosion
Perturbations	disturbances of soil and vegetation from the actions of wind, fire, ice, insects, diseases and humans acting alone, in combination or in sequence
Physiography	the surface features of the earth, and the materials they are composed of
Refugium	an isolated area where, typically, major climatic changes have not occurred
Scaling	the measurement of the quantity and quality of logs
Sedimentary	rocks derived from the weathering of other rocks and deposited mainly by water
Serotinous	cones that remain without opening on a tree for one or more years and open only when heat is applied
Silviculture	the application of knowledge and experience in the art, science and business of the harvesting, establishment, tending and protection of forests
Site preparation	disturbance, primarily of the forest floor and upper mineral soil, to facilitate the

	establishment and early growth of desired species
Slash	tree tops and branches left on the ground after logging or other disturbances
Stand	a community of trees uniform in composition, structure, age or other condition which are distinguishable from other adjacent communities
Succession	the sequential change in plant and animal communities on a specific area
Surficial	pertaining to the earth's surface
Sustainability	the management of resources to meet society's present needs without compromising the needs of future generations
Talus	a mass of rock fragments on the side or at the foot of a cliff or slope
Till	the heterogeneous mixture of rocks, boulders, stones, sands, silt and clay deposited by glaciers. When deposited on the surface as the ice advanced the till is termed basal or subglacial; if deposited as the ice retreated it is termed ablation or supraglacial
Topography	the form or configuration of the earth's surface
Varves	alternating layers, usually of silt and clay, laid down periodically as deposits in lakes
Volcanic	fine-grained rocks produced from the action of volcanoes
Waferboard	a board composed of uniform wafers of wood cut from roundwood, bonded by resins after the application of heat and pressure
Windthrows	trees which are blown down by wind; the soil brought up by the roots of these trees forms mounds, which provide evidence that windthrow occurred even long after the tree has decomposed

K. A. Armson

XII

Botanical Names

American beech	*Fagus grandifolia* Ehrh.
American chestnut	*Castanea dentata* (Marsh.) Borkh.
Ashes	
Black ash	*Fraxinus nigra* Marsh.
Blue ash	*Fraxinus quadrangulata* Michx.
Red ash	*Fraxinus pennsylvanica* Marsh.
White ash	*Fraxinus americana* L.
Balsam fir	*Abies balsamea* (L.) Mill.
Basswood	*Tilia americana* L.
Birches	
Cherry birch	*Betula lenta* L.
Gray birch	*Betula populifolia* Marsh.
White birch	*Betula papyrifera* Marsh.
Yellow birch	*Betula alleghaniensis* Britt.
Black gum	*Nyssa sylvatica* Marsh.
Blueberries	*Vaccinium spp.*
Buckthorn	*Rhamnus cathartica* L.
Cherries and Plums	
Black cherry	*Prunus serotina* Ehrh.
Choke cherry	*Prunus virginiana* L. var. *virginiana*
Pin cherry	*Prunus pensylvanica* L. f.
American plum	*Prunus americana* Marsh.
Canada	*Prunus nigra* Ait.
Cucumber-tree (Magnolia)	*Magnolia acuminata* L.
Currants	*Ribes spp.*
Eastern flowering dogwood	*Cornus florida* L.
Eastern hemlock	*Tsuga canadensis* (L.) Carrière
Eastern redcedar	*Juniperus virginiana* L.
Eastern white-cedar	*Thuya occidentalis* L.

Elderberries	*Sambucus spp.*
Elms	
Slippery elm	*Ulmus rubra* Muhl.
Rock elm	*Ulmus thomasii* Sarg.
White elm	*Ulmus americana* L.
Hackberry	*Celtis occidentalis* L.
Hickories	
Bitternut hickory	*Carya cordiformis* (Wangenh.) K. Koch
Red hickory	*Carya glabra* (Mill.) Sweet var. *odorata* (Marsh.) Little
Shagbark hickory	*Carya ovata* (Mill.) K. Koch
Shellbark hickory	*Carya laciniosa* Michx. f.
Ironwood (hop-hornbeam)	*Ostrya virginiana* (Mill.) K. Koch
Kentucky coffeetree	*Gymnocladus dioicus* (L.) K. Koch
Maples	
Black maple	*Acer nigrum* Michx.
Manitoba maple	*Acer negundo* L.
Mountain maple	*Acer spicatum* Lamb.
Red maple	*Acer rubrum* L.
Silver maple	*Acer saccharinum* L.
Striped maple	*Acer pensylvanicum* L.
Sugar maple	*Acer saccharum* Marsh.
Mountain-ash	
American mountain-ash	*Sorbus americana* Marsh.
Showy mountain-ash	*Sorbus decora* (Sarg.) C.K Schneid.
Oaks	
Black oak	*Quercus velutina* Lam.
Bur oak	*Quercus macrocarpa* Michx.
Chinquapin oak	*Quercus muehlenbergii* Engelm.
Dwarf chinquapin oak	*Quercus prinoides* Willd.
Northern pin oak	*Quercus ellipsoidalis* E.J. Hill
Pin oak	*Quercus palustris* Muenchh.
Red oak	*Quercus rubra* L.
Shumard oak	*Quercus shumardii* Buckl.
Swamp white oak	*Quercus bicolor* Willd.
White oak	*Quercus alba* L.
Papaw	*Asimina triloba* (L.) Dunal
Pines	
Eastern white pine	*Pinus strobus* L.
Jack pine	*Pinus banksiana* Lamb.
Pitch pine	*Pinus rigida* Mill.

K. A. Armson

Red pine	*Pinus resinosa* Ait.
Scots pine	*Pinus sylvestris* L.
Poplars	
Balsam poplar	*Populus balsamifera* L.
Eastern cottonwood	*Populus deltoides* Bartr. ex Marsh. ssp. *deltoides*
Largetooth aspen	*Populus grandidentata* Michx.
Trembling aspen	*Populus tremuloides* Michx.
Redbud	*Cercis canadensis* L.
Serviceberries	*Amelanchier spp.*
Sassafras	*Sassafras albidum* (Nutt.) Nees
Spruces	
Black spruce	*Picea mariana* (Mill.) BSP
Norway spruce	*Picea abies* (L.) Karst.
Red spruce	*Picea rubens* Sarg.
White spruce	*Picea glauca* (Moench) Voss
Staghorn sumac	*Rhus typhina* L.
Sycamore	*Platanus occidentalis* L.
Tamarack(eastern larch)	*Larix laricina* (Du Roi) K. Koch
Tulip-tree	*Liriodendron tulipfera* L.
Walnut and Butternut	
Black walnut	*Juglans nigra* L.
Butternut	*Juglans cinerea* L.
Willows	
Bebb willow	*Salix bebbiana* Sarg.
Black willow	*Salix nigra* Marsh.
Pussy willow	*Salix discolor* Muhl.
Shining willow	*Salix lucida* Muhl. ssp. *lucida*

XIII

Footnotes
and *Selected References*

I. INTRODUCTION

- Footnotes

1 Frazer, J.G. 1954 The Golden Bough—A Study in Magic and Religion. Macmillan & Co. London. p.756

2 Our Common Future, 1987. The World Commission on Environment and Development. Oxford Univ. Press. p.400

3 Glossary of Terms of Soil Science 1976. Agriculture Canada, Ottawa. Publication 1459.

II PROLOGUE

- Selected References

Whitchurch Township. Researched and written by the Whitchurch History Book Committee. 1993. Boston Mills Press, Erin, Ontario. p.160 + illus.

- Footnotes

1 This early history is taken directly from, Staley, R.N. "The Staley Woodlot— Raccoons, Recreation and Red Oak Logs". an illustrated booklet published by Mr. Staley.

2 A report on the exploration of the country between Lake Superior and the Red River Settlement. In Appendix 2 to Vol. 16 of the Journal of the Legislative Assembly of the Province of Canada, 1858.

III BEFORE FORESTS

- Selected References

Brown, D.M., G.A.McKay and L.J.Chapman. 1968. The Climate of Southern Ontario Climatological Studies No.5. Canada Meteorological Branch, p.50

Chapman, L.J. and D.F. Putnam. 1966. 2nd ed. The Physiography of Southern Ontario. Univ. Toronto Press, Toronto. p.386.

Chapman, L.J. and M.K.Thomas. 1968. The Climate of Northern Ontario. Climatological studies No.6. Canada Meteorological Branch, p.58

Prest, V.K. 1970. Quaternary geology in Canada, Ch. XII in R.J.E.Douglas(ed.) Geology and Economic Minerals of Canada, p.676–764. Dept. Energy, Mines and Resources, Ottawa.

Sado, E.V. and B.F. Carswell. 1987. Surficial geology of Northern Ontario. Ontario Geological Survey, Map 2518. Min. Northern Dev. And Mines, Toronto.

Terasmae, J. and O.L.Hughes. 1960. Glacial retreat in the North Bay area. Science 131: 1444–6

Tovell, W. M. 1992. (L.Brown, ed.). Guide to the Geology of the Niagara Escarpment. Niagara Escarpment Commission

- Footnotes
1 BP—Before the Present
2 Recent geological investigations indicate that there may have been more than four.
3 McAndrews, J.H. 1984. Late Quaternary climate of Ontario: temperature trends from the fossil pollen p. 319–333, in Quaternary Paleoclimate. Ed. W.C.Mahaney. Geo Astracts, Univ. East Anglia, Norwich
4 Pierpoint, G. and J.L. Farrar. 1962. The water balance of the University of Toronto Forest. Tech. Rep. No.3. Faculty of Forestry, Univ.Toronto. p. 48

IV GREENING UP

- Selected References

Allison, T.D., Moeller, R.E. and M.B.Davis. 1986. Pollen in laminated sediments provides evidence for a mid-Holocene forest pathogen outbreak.. Ecology 67: 1101–1105

Anonymous. 1996. Forest Resources of Ontario. Ontario Ministry of Natural Resources, Toronto and Peterborough. p.86 + illus.

Bennett, K.D. 1987. Holocene history of forest trees in southern Ontario. Can. J. Bot. 65:8:1792–1801

Burns, R.M. and B.H.Honkala, Tech. Coords. 1990. Silvics of North America.: 1 Conifers. Agric. Handbook 654. U.S. Dept. of Agriculture, Forest Service. Washington D.C., p.675

Burns, R.M. and B.H.Honkala, Tech. Coords. 1990. Silvics of North America.: 2 Conifers. Agric. Handbook 654. U.S. Dept. of Agriculture, Forest Service. Washington D.C., p.877

Delcourt, P.A. and H. R. Delcourt. 1987. Long-term Forest Dynamics of the Temperate Forest Zone. Ecological Studies 63. Springer-Verlag, New York. p. 439 + illus.

Farrar, J.L. 1998. Trees in Canada. Fitzhenry & Whiteside, Markham, and Canadian Forest Service, Ottawa. p.502 + illus.

Gordon, A.G. 1996. The sweep of the Boreal in time and space, from forest formations to genes and implications for management. For. Chron.72:19–30

Jacobson Jr. and A. Dieffenbacher-Krall. 1995. White pine and climate change: insights from the past. J. For. 93:7: 39–42

Karrow, P.F. and B.G. Warner. 1990. The geological and biological environment for Human occupation in southern Ontario. p.5–35, in Ellis, C.J. and N. Ferris (eds.) The Archaeology of southern Ontario. Occas. Paper London Chapter, Ontario Archaeological Society. No. 5, p.570

Pielou, E.C. 1991. After the ice age. The return of life to glaciated North America. Univ. Chicago Press, Chicago. p. 366

Ritchie, J.C. 1987. Postglacial vegetation of Canada. Cambridge Univ. Press. Cambridge. p. 178

Rowe, J. S. 1972. Forest Regions of Canada. Canadian Forest Service, Ottawa. p. 172

Webb III, T. 1981. The past 11,000 years of vegetational change in eastern North America. Bioscience 31: 501–506

- Footnotes
1 Bakowsky, W. 1999. Rare vegetation of Ontario: Tallgrass Prairie and Savannah. NHIC Newsletter, Spring, 1999. Ontario Min. Nat. Res. Peterborough.

V THE LIFE AND TIMES OF ONTARIO'S FORESTS
Non-Human
- Selected References

Clayton, J.S., Ehrlich, W.A. Cann, D.B., Day, J.H. and I.B. Marshall. 1977.Soils of Canada. Vols. 1 and 2. Can. Dept. Agric. Ottawa.

Johnson, W.T. and H.H. Lyon. 1976 Insects that feed on trees and shrubs. Cornell University Press, Ithaca. p. 464 + illus.

Martineau, R. 1984. Insects harmful to forest trees.Canadian Forest Service, Ottawa. p.261 + illus.

Sinclair, W.S., H.H. Lyon and W.T. Johnson. 1987. Diseases of trees and shrubs. Cornell University Press, Ithaca. p. 574 + illus.

- Footnotes

1   Whitney, R.D. 1988. The Hidden Enemy. Great Lakes Forestry Centre, Canadian Forest Service, Sault Ste. Marie. p.35 + illus.

Human
- Selected References

Biggar, H.P. (ed.) 1936. The Champlain Journals II. The Champlain Society, University Of Toronto.

Bowman, Irene. 1979. The Draper Site: Historical accounts of vegetation in Pickering and Markham Townships with special reference to the significance of a large even-aged stand adjacent to the site. P. 47–58 in Settlement Patterns of the Draper and White Sites. Hayden, B. (ed.) Dept. Archaeology, Publ. No. 6. Simon Fraser Univ. Burnaby, B.C.

Burden, E.T., McAndrews, J.H. and Norris, G. 1986. Palynology of Indian and European Forest clearance and farming in lake sediment cores from Awenda Provincial Park, Ontario. Can.J.Earth Sci. 23:43–54

Burden, E.T., McAndrews, J.H. and Norris, G. 1986. Geochemical indicators in lake sediment of upland erosion caused by indian and European farming, Awenda Provincial Park, Ontario. Can.J.Earth Sci. 23:55–65

Ellis, C.J. and N. Ferris (eds.) 1990. The Archaeology of southern Ontario. Occas. Publ. London Chapter, Ont. Arch. Soc. No.5. p.570

Harris, R. Cole. (ed.) 1987. Historical Atlas of Canada. Vol. I, from the beginning to 1800. Univ. Toronto Press, Toronto. p. 198 + illus.

Heidenreich, C.E. 1971. Huronia, a history of Ontario's indians from 1600 to 1650. McClelland and Stewart, Toronto. p.337

Sagard, Father Gabriel, 1939. The Long Journey to the Country of the Hurons.edited by B. M. Wrong. transl. H. H. Langdon. The Champlain Society. Facsimile edition, Greenwood Press, 1968

Wright, J.V. 1995. A History of the Native People of Canada. Vol. 1. Archaeological Survey of Canada, Paper 152. Can. Mus. Civilization, Ottawa. p.564

- Footnotes

2   Much of the information describing the Hurons is drawn from Heidenreich, C.E. 1971

3   I am indebted to Dr. William Finlayson who provided these details of the Draper site

4   Dr. William Finlayson—personal communication

5   Campbell, I.D. and J.H.McAndrews, 1991. Cluster analysis of late Holocene pollen trends in Ontario. Can.J.Bot. 69:8:1719–1730.

1650 to 1850 Waterways and War
- Selected References

Craig, G.M. 1963. Upper Canada. The Formative Years, 1784–1841. McClelland and Stewart, Toronto. p.315

Honer, T.G. 1998. Without Fear or Favour: culling & scaling timber in Canada 1762–1992. T.G. Honer & Associates, Victoria. p213 + illus.

Lambert, R.S. with Paul Pross. 1967. Renewing Nature's Wealth. Ontario Dept. Lands & Forests. Toronto. p.630

Lower, A.R.M. 1938. The North American Assault on the Canadian Forest. Toronto, The Ryerson Press. p.377

Lower, A.R.M. 1973. Great Britain's Woodyard. McGill-Queen's Press, Montréal, p. 271

Reaman, G.L. 1957. The Trail of the Black Walnut. McClelland & Stewart, Toronto, p. 256

- <u>Footnotes</u>

6 Johnson, L.A. 1973. History of the County of Ontario, 1615–1875. The Corporation of the County of Ontario, Whitby. p. 386

7 Lambert, R.S. with Paul Pross. 1967. Renewing Nature's Wealth. Ontario Department of Lands and   Forests, Toronto. p.630

8 Scaling is the measurement or estimation of the quantity or quality of felled timber

1851 to 1920 Lumber, Newsprint and the Beginnings of Conservation

- <u>Footnotes</u>

9 MacCrimmon, H.R. 1977. Animals, Man and Change, alien and extinct wildlife of Ontario. McClelland and Stewart, Toronto. p.160

10 Racey, G.D. and T. Armstrong. 2000. Woodland caribou range occupancy in northwestern Ontario: past and present. Rangifer Special Issue No.12

11 Forest Resources Inventory of Ontario,1996. Ontario Ministry of Natural Resources, Toronto, p.86

12 The Forest Resources of Ontario, 1963. Ontario Department of lands and Forests, Toronto, p.107

13 Appendix, Annual Report of the Clerk of Forestry for the Province of Ontario 1897, p.64.

14 Assessor for Logan Twp., Perth County, in Clerk of Forestry Report for 1886

15 Larson, B.M., J.L.Riley, E.A.Snell and Godschalk, H.G. 1999. The Woodland Heritage of Southern Ontario, a study of ecological change, distibution and significance. Federation of Ontario Naturalists, Toronto. p.262

16 Wightman, W.R. and N.M.Wightman, 1997. The Land Between: Northwestern Ontario Resource Development. Unv.Toronto Press, Table 2.1

17 Niven, A. in Champlain Society 1973. Thunder Bay District, 1821–1892, ed. Elizabeth Arthur.

18 for a fuller account on the Dingley tariff see, Angus, J.T. 1990. A Deo Victoria. The Story of the Georgian Bay Lumber Company 1871–1942. Ontario Heritage Foundation, Local History Series #2, Severn Publications Ltd., Thunder Bay. pages 231–233.

19 Fernow, B.E. 1912. Conditions in the Clay Belt of New Ontario. Report to the Commission on Conservation, Ottawa. 1913

20 Report of the Royal Commission on Forestry Protection in Ontario, 1899, p.29

21 Phipps, R.W. 1883 Report on the Necessity of Preserving and Replanting Forests, Gov. Ontario. p.138

22 Zavitz, E.J. 1909. Report on the Reforestation of Waste Lands in Southern Ontario. Ontario Dept. of Agriculture, Toronto. 28p.

23 Pross, A.P. 1967. The development of a forest policy: a study of the Ontario Department of Lands and Forests. Ph.D. thesis, Dept. Political Economy, University of Toronto.

24 1996, A Sustainable Forest Management System: Guidance Document, CAN/CSA-Z808-96, and Specifications Document, CAN/CSA-Z809-96. Canadian Standards Association, Toronto

1921 to 1950 Forestry Begins Then Stalls

- Footnotes

25 Johnston, R.N and J.F. Sharpe. 1923. Report of the James Bay Forest Survey, Moose River Lower Basin. 1922. Forestry Branch, Ontario Department of Lands and Forests. Toronto. p.16 + maps.

26 Sharpe, J.F. and J.A.Brodie, 1931. The Forest Resources of Ontario 1930. Forestry Branch, Ontario Department of Lands and Forests, Toronto. p.60 + maps.

27 For an account of Johnston's role and the development of the Ontario Provincial Air Service, see West, B. 1974. The Firebirds. Ontario Ministry of Natural Resources, Toronto. p. 258 + illus.

28 for an account of the Commission and the reasons for its demise see Gillis, R.P., and Roach, T.R., 1986. Lost Initiatives. The Forest History Society, Greenwood Press, Westport, CT. p.326

29 From information made available to me by Abitibi-Consolidated Inc. staff at Iroquois Falls. A comprehensive account can be found in: Kuhlberg, M. 1999. "We have sold "Forestry" to the Management of the Company": Abitibi Power and Paper Company's Forestry Initiatives in Ontario, 1919–1929. J.Can. Studies, 34:3:187–209.

30 Much of the information relating to the forest conditions following logging is drawn from, Hosie, R.C. 1953. Forest Regeneration in Ontario. Forestry Bull. No.2. Univ. Toronto Press, Toronto.

31 Coons, C.F. 1992. The Alligator Steam Warping Tug. For. Chron. 68: 594–597. Also unpublished mss. of the same title by Coons, C.F.

32 Report of the Ontario Royal Commission on Forestry, 1947. The King's Printer, Toronto. p.196 + illus. and maps.

33 Plosz, A.J. 1988. Q&O Our Story.. The Québec and Ontario Paper Company Ltd., St. Catharines, Ontario. p.56 + illus

34 Report of the Select Committee on Conservation, Ontario Government, Toronto. p. 188 + illus. & maps

35 Most of the information on forest pests for this period is taken from: Turner, K.B. 1965 A History of Investigations into and Control of Pests of Forest Trees in Ontario. Unpublished mss. Ontario Department of Lands and Forests, Toronto.

1951 to 1980 Forestry Regenerated

- Footnotes

36 Sharpe, J.F. 1947. Progress of Forestry in Ontario. p.492–504 in Proc. Soc. Amer. Foresters Mtg. 1947

37 A more comprehensive account of the development of forest management units is in: Bruce, D.S. 1986, The Establishment of Forest Management Units in Ontario and their Historic Origin. Unpublished mss. Ontario Ministry of Natural Resources, Toronto

38 A Report on the Status of Forest Regeneration, 1992. The Ontario Independent Forest Audit Committee, Ontario Ministry of Natural Resources, Sault Ste. Marie. p.117 + illus.

39 Report of the Forestry Study Unit. 1967. Ontario Department of Lands and Forests, Toronto. p.309

40 Townsend, E.Ray. 1996. Algonquin Forestry Authority ...A 20 Year History. The Algonquin Forestry Authority, Huntsville. p.72 + illus.

41 Forest Production Policy Options for Ontario, 1972. Ontario Ministry of Natural Resources, Toronto. p.81

42 Armson, K.A. 1976. Forest Management in Ontario. Ministry of Natural Resources, Toronto. p.172

43 The statistical information about private land forests is derived mainly from, Private Land Forests—A Public Resource.1982. Ontario Ministry of Natural Resources, Toronto. p.161 + Appendix

44 Forest Management Agreements 1988. Ontario Ministry of Natural Resources, Toronto. p.13 + illus.

1981 to 2000 Forests and Urban Society—Forestry's Challenge

* Selected References

Armson, K.A., W.R.Grinnell, and F.C.Robinson. 2000. Chapter 1. History of Reforestation, in Regenerating the Canadian Forest: Principles and Practice for Ontario. Fitzhenry & Whiteside, Toronto.

Burgar, R.J. 1983. Forest Land-Use Evolution in Ontario's Upper Great Lakes Basin, Chapter 11, p.177–193, in The Great Lakes Forest—an environmental and social history, ed. Susan L.Flader.Univ. Minn. Press. Minneapolis, p.336

Howe, C.D. and J.H.White. 1913. Trent Watershed Survey—a reconnaissance. Commission of Conservation, Canada, Ottawa. p.156 + maps

Lambert, R.S. 1967. Renewing Nature's Wealth. Ontario Department of Lands and Forests. Toronto. p.630 + illus.

Nelles, H.V. 1974. The Politics of Development—Forests, Mines and Hydro-Electric Power in Ontario 1849–1941. Macmillan of Canada, Toronto, p. 514

Radforth, I. 1987. Bushworkers and Bosses: logging in northern Ontario, 1900–1980. Univ.Toronto Press, Toronto. p. 360

Schull, J. 1978. Ontario since 1867. Ontario Historical Studies Series. McLelland and Stewart, Toronto. p.400 + illus.

Silversides, C.Ross. 1997.Broadaxe to Flying Shear.The mechanization of forest harvesting east of the Rockies. National Museum of Science and Technology, Ottawa. p.174 + illus.

Whitton, C. 1943. A Hundred Years a-Felling. Gillies Bros. Braeside. P. 172

Wightman, W.R. and N.M. Wightman, 1997. The Land Between: Northwestern Ontario Resource Development, 1800 to the 1990s. Univ.Toronto Press Toronto. p.566

* Footnotes

45 Borczon, E.L. 1982. Evergreen Challenge—The Agreement Forest Story. Ministry of Natural Resources, Toronto. p.60 + illus.

46 Renewable Resource Futures, Report of the Research and Development Steering Committee (Walmsley Report). 1984. Ontario Ministry of Natural Resources, Toronto. p.53

47 Forestry Research Survey and Research Funding and Expenditures in Ontario for 1984–85 and 1985–86. 1986. The Longwoods Research Group Ltd., Toronto. unpubl. p.50 + Appendices

48 Reasons for Decision and Decision, Class Environmental Assessment by the Ministry of Natural Resources for Timber Management on Crown lands in Ontario. EA-87-02, Before: Anne Koven and Elie Martel. April, 1994. p. 561

49 Baskerville, G.L. 1986. An Audit of Management of the Crown Forests of Ontario. Ontario Ministry of Natural Resources, Toronto. p. 97

K. A. Armson

50 Survey of Artifical Regeneration in Northern Ontario (SOARS 1). 1987. Unpublished mss. Ontario Ministry of Natural Resources, Toronto

51 Regeneration is judged "Free-to-Grow" when it meets all of the criteria for: a) stocking (amount and distribution of regeneration); b) minimum height; and c) is essentially free from competing vegetation.

52 FFT—Forests for Tomorrow, a coalition of several groups including the Federation of Ontario Naturalists, the Sierra Club of Ontario, and the Wildlands League.

53 Ontario Forest Policy Panel, 1993. Diversity: Forests, People, Communities—A Comprehensive Forest Policy Framework for Ontario. Queen's Printer for Ontario, Toronto. p.147

54 Sustainable Forests—A National Commitment. 1992. Canadian Council of Forest Ministers, Hull, QC. p.51

55 Conserving Ontario's Old Growth Forest Ecosystems. Highlights and Recommendations of the Final Report of the Old Growth Forests Policy Advisory Committee, 1994. Ontario Ministry of Natural Resources, Toronto. p. 32.

56 Day, R.J. and J.V.Carter, 1991. The Ecology of the Temagami Forest: based on a photointerpretive survey and the Forest Resources Inventory of Temagami District. Ontario Ministry of Natural Resources, Sudbury. p.88.

57 Day, R.J. and J.V.Carter, 1991. Stand Structure and Successional Development of the White and rRed Pine Communities in the Temagami Forest. Ontario Ministry of Natural Resources, Sudbury. p. 203

58 Chris Hodgson,, Minister of Natural Resources, in Lands for Life, 1997, Ministry of Natural resources, Toronto. p. 11.

CHANGING VALUES AND FUTURE FORESTS

• Footnotes

1 Report of the First Annual Meeting of the Canadian Forestry Association, Ottawa, March 8,1900, reprinted March 1975 in honour of the 75th Anniversary of the Association. p.32 + illus.

2 Fensom, K.G. 1972. Expanding Horizons. A History of the Canadian Institute of Forestry-Institut du Canada. Canadian Institute of Forestry-Institut Forestier du Canada, Ottawa. p.547

3 Hodgins, B.W. and J. Benedickson. 1989. The Temagami Experience: Recreation, Resources, and Aboriginal Rights in the Northern Ontario Wilderness. Univ.Toronto Press. p. 370 + illus.

K. A. Armson

K. A. Armson

K. A. Armson

white ash, 71
white birch, 55, 67, 91, 144, 159, 164
white elm, 53, 70
white oak, 56, 69
white pine weevil, 93, 94, 141
White River nursery, 154
white spruce, 47, 48, 49, 55, 59, 61, 127, 130
white-tailed deer, 64, 67, 118, 119
Wildlands League, 183
wild turkey, 118
Wildman, C.J., 172
willow, 55
Wilmot, Samuel, 118
windthrow, 89
Winnipeg, 23, 127, 129
Wisconsin, 30, 33, 47, 51
woodland caribou, 119, 175
Woodlands Improvement Act (1966), 166
Woodlands Improvement Agreement (WIA), 164, 167
Woodland peoples, 103
woodlots, 16
wood pulp, 127
World Wildlife Fund Canada, 183

Y

yellow birch, 55, 67, 161, 162, 164, 190
Yonge Street, 113, 115
York, 113, 115

Z

Zavitz, E.J., 131, 132, 133, 134, 141, 143